Maximum Effort -
Maximum Performance!

Bill Ezzy

Calll M

LEARNING LEADERSHIP

Applying Supersonic Jet Flying Principles
to Business and Life

BILL HENSLEY   **COLLEEN HENSLEY**

GREENLEAF
BOOK GROUP PRESS

Published by Greenleaf Book Group Press
Austin, Texas
www.gbgpress.com

This book is in no way affiliated with, or endorsed by, the United States Air Force, The Department of Defense, or any other governmental or military agency or organization.

Names, characters, businesses, organizations, places, events, and incidents are either a product of the authors' imagination or are used fictitiously. Any resemblance to actual persons, living or dead, events, or locales is entirely coincidental.

This publication is designed to provide accurate and authoritative information in regard to the subject matter covered. The authors have made their best efforts in preparing this book, however they make no representations or warranties regarding its accuracy, completeness, or fitness of use in a particular situation. This book is sold with the understanding that the publisher and authors are not engaged in rendering legal, accounting, or any other professional services or advice. If legal advice or other expert assistance is required, the services of a competent professional should be sought.

Readers should be aware that Internet Web sites offered as citations and/or sources for further information may have changed or disappeared between the time this book was written and when it is read.

Distributed by Greenleaf Book Group LLC

For ordering information or special discounts for bulk purchases, please contact Greenleaf Book Group LLC at PO Box 91869, Austin, TX 78709, 512.891.6100.

Design and composition by Greenleaf Book Group LLC

Publisher's Cataloging-In-Publication Data
(Prepared by The Donohue Group, Inc.)

Hensley, Bill.
   The pilot : learning leadership : applying supersonic jet flying principles to business and life / by Bill Hensley and Colleen Hensley. — 1st ed.
     p. ; cm.
   ISBN: 978-1-60832-075-2
   1. Leadership. 2. Success in business. 4. Allegories. I. Hensley, Colleen. II. Title.
HD57.7 .H46 2011
658.4/092   2010941626

Part of the Tree Neutral® program, which offsets the number of trees consumed in the production and printing of this book by taking proactive steps, such as planting trees in direct proportion to the number of trees used: www.treeneutral.com

TreeNeutral

Printed in the United States of America on acid-free paper

11 12 13 14 15   10 9 8 7 6 5 4 3 2 1

First Edition

THIS BOOK IS DEDICATED TO OUR SON, LOGAN, WHO
INSPIRES US AND MAKES US PROUD.

Contents

PREFACE

You are about to embark on a journey that will cause you to look at everything you do from a completely different perspective—a perspective that is simple yet astonishingly significant. Imagine what the world would be like if people did their job, ran their business, and orchestrated their relationships as if their life depended on it. The story you are about to read will give you a view into that world, because it does exist. It's the world of flying supersonic jets. In this book we tell a story of how a group of ordinary people do the extraordinary—earn their wings as supersonic jet pilots.

The significance of this process is not to learn how to fly high-performance jets, but rather to embody and practice the lifelong lessons that accompany such an experience. Indeed, these lessons can be carried forward, and built upon, for a lifetime. These are the lessons that you will be able to apply to your life and business. Your business could be anything from a large corporation, to an entrepreneurial enterprise, to a service organization of first-responders, and virtually everything in between. The result will be an exponential growth in your personal and professional leadership and followership effectiveness.

Over the past few decades we've seen firsthand how such skills can transfer from the cockpit to the business world. We (both Colleen and Bill) have had the honor of serving our country as United States Air Force pilots. We flew aircraft that ranged from the supersonic T-38 Talon to the four-engine worldwide jet transport, the C-141 Starlifter. After flying as Air Force pilots, we became commercial airline pilots. We flew domestically and internationally in a large number of Boeing jets that included the 727, 737, 757, and 767.

We became students of followership and leadership in arenas that ranged from Air Force flying squadrons to the massive organizations of commercial airlines that employed tens of thousands of people. Since leaving the cockpit, we have enjoyed business success by founding a profitable company and becoming investors in various start-up ventures.

Using our experience in the world of aviation and the world of business, we have developed the three elements of this book: Mastery of Performance, Mach One Followership, and Center Seat Leadership. They are the essential and sequential concepts of learning leadership, and they have countless personal and business applications.

In this book you'll be able to experience these elements of leadership through the eyes of student pilots and instructors in the environment of supersonic jet pilot training. The story is fictional, yet based in reality. At the end of the chapters, you'll find discussions of selected concepts and principles. Borrowing a term from the aviation world, we call these end-of-chapter discussions *debriefs*.

After reading this book, you will be prepared to do the extraordinary. The greater the magnitude of the challenges you face, the greater the necessity that you use the ideas illustrated in our story and discussed in the debriefs. Our concepts and principles have been incubated in the cockpit and burnished in the business world; now they're ready for you to implement.

MASTERY OF PERFORMANCE

1

WELCOME TO TIGER FLIGHT

The term "razor sharp" could have been created solely to describe Captain Neil Williamson, a squadron check pilot in the supersonic T-38. Both Neil and the jet were known to be fast, unforgiving, and intimidating.

Neil clicked the controller in his hand. The image of an upside-down jet performing aerobatics flashed on the screen behind him. "You are about to begin your six-month sprint to the finish," he said, meeting as many eyes in the room as possible with perfect posture and a clear command of the environment. "It's your sprint to earn the wings of a United States Air Force jet pilot."

All twenty-five student pilots, twenty-four men and one woman, looked directly at him from the rows of desks. Their number was down from the thirty that had started the program more than five months earlier. Neil signaled for the lights to be turned back on. "Congratulations on getting through Phase I and Phase II of Undergraduate Pilot Training, or UPT, but your toughest challenge lies ahead," he said. "You've been here at Whiley Air Force Base for a while now. You've completed a month of academics, and spent five months flying the T-37, or the Tweet as we call it. Starting tomorrow, you'll be assigned to Tiger Flight in the T-38 squadron across the street. The T-38 is officially designated the Talon, but around here we call it the White Rocket."

Neil sat on the edge of the table next to him. "I know your stories. You all have a college degree and you're all commissioned officers. You made it through Officer Training School, ROTC, or the Air Force Academy. You're first-place finishers and used to winning. I have a news flash for you. The jet you're about to strap into doesn't care about any of that. It's an equal-opportunity destroyer of careers, or lives, if you make a mistake. The White Rocket plays for keeps if you screw up—no second chances like in the Tweet."

The students looked around at one another. Neil knew that they had already been through more than most could handle. "Now comes the real test. Will you be able to master flying the White Rocket to the standards set by the U.S. Air Force? Once you climb into the cockpit of a jet that can break the speed of sound, there is no doubt that some of you will fall by the wayside. Whether you make the cut will depend on how well you prepare, how much you practice, and then how well you perform on your checkrides. Before long, we'll know who's doing what it takes to get through the second half of the program—and who's not. Remember, the carrot you're chasing is your ultimate class ranking. The higher you finish, the greater the chance you'll have of getting your first choice of assignment when you graduate . . . *if* you graduate. You may want to fly a front-line fighter or troop-and-cargo hauler, or be an instructor. Don't even think about that until you prove to your instructors that you can handle everything they throw at you."

Neil checked his watch, a habit reflecting the attention he paid to the smallest detail. "You already know that Undergraduate Pilot Training is like fifty-two consecutive weeks of finals in college. You'll get to a point where you'll think that your mind and body have taken all they can, and then you'll simply have to demand more of yourself than you ever thought possible." A jet flew directly overhead the briefing room, rattling the window blinds, punctuating Neil's statement. "Flying the T-38 requires the absolute mastery of a multitude of skills, some you haven't even imagined yet. You have to want this more than anything you've ever wanted in your life. It'll be the toughest thing you ever do—but also the most rewarding if you survive. More than that, it'll be what defines you; a clear statement of what you stand for and what you're capable of achieving throughout the rest of your life."

He paused for a moment to let the thought sink into the impressionable minds of the young lieutenants filling the seats of the briefing room. "I'm sure you all have questions. First, though, I'll go over some specifics of the program. To earn the honor of wearing those silver pilot wings on your chest, you'll need to continue to do what you've been doing, only now, you'll need to master flying a supersonic jet. You'll also continue to develop your leadership skills, while increasing your understanding of what it takes, first, to be a great follower. You don't graduate from your commissioning source as a general, and there's a reason for that. You need to learn how to follow before you can learn how to lead.

"You've all learned takeoffs, landings, stalls, and aerobatics. You've learned to fly using outside references—*contact flying*. You've learned to fly by referring only to instruments inside the cockpit—*instrument flying*. And finally . . . you've learned how to fly next to another jet in *formation flying*. You'll do the same in the White Rocket, only in a blindingly fast, slippery, and much less forgiving jet that will eat you alive if you lose focus for even a second."

Neil paused to take a sip from a cup of coffee as he surveyed the room once again. "The basic structure of the training syllabus is the same as you experienced in Tweets. Complete a portion of the program and you'll be sent down to Check Section to fly with a check pilot to show him if you're ready to move on to the next phase of the program. Just as you're used to, it'll start with an oral ground evaluation; bust that, and you won't even get to the jet. Being a check pilot, I can tell you that we will expect that you pretty much know every line of your flight manual and the reason you perform every step of your ground and flight procedures. As long as you have that down, you'll have nothing to worry about."

After hearing a few gulps from the lieutenants sitting before him, Neil noticed a hand pop up from the back of the room.

"Whose hand is up in the back row?" Neil asked sternly.

"Sir, I'm Lieutenant Clark."

"What's your question, Lieutenant?"

"If we do bust a checkride, what's the procedure for our re-check?"

"It's the same as you had in the other squadron," Neil answered. "You'll get a training ride or two and then a re-check. If you bust the re-check, you'll find the brightest spotlight you ever imagined focused on the center of your forehead. Basically, if you are given another chance after that, you're only a few rides away from being booted from the program—washing out."

Neil checked his watch again. "We've got a lot more ground to cover in the twenty-three minutes we have left," he said, more as a reminder for himself than the students. He routinely used exact measurements to get the students accustomed to how precise they would need to be in this advanced stage of training.

For the first time, a slight smile crossed Neil's face. "Now, I can tell you that I've spoken to pilots who've spent decades in the Air Force and still call the T-38 their favorite jet. You already know that it's a supersonic jet with two afterburning engines. But here's something to write home about. Besides taking you faster than the speed of sound, this jet will take you *up* faster than anything you've ever experienced or imagined.

"Can anyone tell me how long it takes a typical airliner to climb to cruising altitude?" Neil zeroed in on Lieutenant Chatsworth as his hand went up.

"Probably a good twenty to twenty-five minutes to get to thirty thousand feet," Chatsworth replied.

"That's correct . . . around twenty-five minutes. The White Rocket, on the other hand, has an initial climb rate in excess of thirty thousand feet *per minute*. In fact, shortly after it entered service as an operational jet, it held four international time-to-climb records. Now, that's something you can write home about. That's why they call it the White Rocket."

"Hooyah!" came a holler from the third row back.

"You like the sound of that, Lieutenant?"

"Yes, sir, I do," answered Lieutenant Gerry Barrett. His smile and laugh paved the way for a few more chest-pounding vocals that released the tension that had been building in the room.

Neil cracked another half smile. "Most students recall their first T-38 flight as little more than a blur. Before you know it, you'll be leveling off and feeling like you've left your mind back on the runway."

Gerry let fly another testosterone-filled hoot; several others followed.

"On a more serious note, consider yourselves warned. The Tweet is very forgiving of pilot mistakes. If you think of it as a nice stable four-door sedan . . . then the T-38 is a Lamborghini at full throttle on a wet roadway. There's no time or room for errors. The point is, you can never let your guard down. If you do, that's precisely when this jet will bite you."

Neil checked the clock on the wall instead of his watch. He ran his fingers through his thick, yet regulation-cut, dark brown hair, and asked for any further questions.

"Captain Williamson, how many training missions will we fly in the T-38 and how many checkrides are there in the program?" asked Lieutenant Dewey Clark.

"As in the Tweet, you'll have three checkrides. You'll fly around twenty syllabus flights before your first checkride, which will be your contact check. On that checkride, you'll demonstrate proficiency in aerobatics, stalls, and takeoffs and landings. Then, you'll fly about thirty more flights to prepare for your formation check. If you make it that far, you'll then fly another eighteen to twenty instrument and cross-country flights to prepare for your navigation check. Your navigation check consists of flying to another base and back on instruments. For that checkride, you'll be in the backseat and pull forward a curtain—*the bag*— that'll completely block your view of anything outside the cockpit. It's like flying in a dense cloud from takeoff to touchdown. You'll also have some simulator missions thrown in here and there, but that's the T-38 program in a nutshell."

Lieutenant Clark followed up with another question. "And what kind of hours will we be putting in during the 38 phase?"

"What kind of hours are you used to putting in over in Tweets, Lieutenant?" asked Neil as he cocked his head, surprised at the question.

"Around twelve hours a day," answered Lieutenant Clark.

"You'd better add a few to that number starting tomorrow. And if you're not already there, you'd better get used to reporting at three a.m. one week, then eleven a.m. the next week. The Air Force hasn't quite adopted the latest circadian-rhythm studies," replied Neil, noticing a few chuckles throughout the room.

"And don't expect the enemy to care about what time you have to get up during a war," Neil said with all seriousness. The chuckling stopped.

Finally someone spoke up with a question that, Neil knew from experience, ran like an undercurrent through everyone's mind.

"Lieutenant Macfadden?" He pointed to the only female pilot in the flight.

"What are some of the main reasons that students wash out of the T-38 phase of the program?" she asked.

Neil pondered the question and considered how to condense all the reasons into a short, sensible answer. "They vary. I'm sure your class is like others. Some couldn't take the pace of academics, some couldn't master certain maneuvers in the jet, and a few, no doubt, were medically disqualified. But some of you may not have what it takes to fly formation at the level required in 38s. Others may forget that—even above and beyond being pilots—you're officers, first and foremost. You've all figured out by now that being an officer comes with standards and expectations that you don't set aside when you hang up your uniform at the end of the day. You're expected to uphold those standards at *all times*. If you don't, the Air Force doesn't want you at the controls of a multimillion-dollar jet." Neil gave them a few seconds to absorb the impact of what he was saying. "And, last but not least, even though you've made it this far, one or two of you may still choose SIE—self-initiated elimination. I know that everyone thinks 'no way, never, not me.' But the challenges of being an officer and a T-38 pilot are more than most people can live with day in and day out."

Neil lowered his head slightly and stared at the students in front of him. "Last question, Lieutenant Logan."

"Captain Williamson, when you were going through pilot training, what was *your* biggest challenge in the T-38 phase?"

Taken aback by the personal nature of the question, Neil began with a stock answer about balancing his time and studying harder than ever, but then he caught himself. "Everything comes so much faster in this phase," he said. "You have to be ridiculously prepared. While this was clearly where I wanted to be, I look back on it now and realize I had to get comfortable being uncomfortable for fifty-two weeks. Dealing with the increased pace of the program and the unforgiving nature of the White Rocket was the challenge."

Looking up, he shifted the conversation away from his own experience. "One wrong move and you'll make the evening news. Learn to be uncomfortable and perform brilliantly, regardless."

Neil walked to the side of the room and took a glance out the window. He had reached his limit of being cooped up in a classroom, and the personal nature of the last question irritated him even more. He watched a T-38 fly overhead and realized that giving briefings such as this one was part of the price he had to pay to fly the White Rocket.

Scratching his chin as he walked back to the front of the room, he continued his presentation. "Okay, here's what it all comes down to. You've made it halfway through Undergraduate Pilot Training. The phase that you'll begin tomorrow will be exponentially more challenging than what you just completed. If this training were open-ended with an unlimited number of flights and bananas, we could get a monkey through the program. Unfortunately we don't have an unlimited supply of either. Seriously, though, the number of flights in the training syllabus is just about at an all-time low right now. Bust your hump every second that you're awake and dream about systems and procedures when you're asleep, and you'll have a chance to get your wings. Ease up or lose focus before the finish line and it'll all be over for you in the blink of an eye."

Neil signaled a student at the back of the room to switch off a row of lights. An oversize image of a young officer receiving shiny silver pilot wings at a graduation ceremony flashed on the screen. "The statistics have been fairly consistent through the years. There are twenty-five of you sitting here today. No doubt about it . . . a few of you have a good chance of not being at the graduation ceremony six months from now. It is your job to make sure that you're among the ones who will be there."

CHAPTER ONE DEBRIEF

THE SETUP

The greater danger for most of us lies not in setting our aim too high and falling short; but in setting our aim too low, and achieving our mark.

MICHELANGELO, ITALIAN RENAISSANCE ARTIST

In The Pilot—Learning Leadership, *we provide debriefs after every chapter except the last, which is followed by the Afterword. We review and expand upon the core concepts that our characters experience in the story. These concepts reflect the business, leadership, and life practices we have brought from the aviation world to the business world. We invite you to take the process one step further by thinking about the question that is posed at the end of each debrief. If you desire clarification of some of the terms used throughout the book, please reference the glossary.*

Imagine flying faster than the speed of sound, performing aerobatics, and experiencing the force of gravity to the point that your body weighs one thousand pounds. Imagine learning to do this merely months after your first flight in a supersonic jet. Then imagine teaching it to others months after your own training is complete. This is not only possible, but commonplace, in the world of supersonic jet training. It is through a crucible of intense and focused learning that it becomes a reality.

It's important that you understand from the outset that the setting of this story is supersonic jet training; yet the lessons learned from such an experience and how they transfer beyond the cockpit are the point of this book. The long list of concepts and many of the acronyms we discuss are not literally taught in pilot training. Rather, they are concepts that we discovered years later and articulate in this book. As you progress through the story and debriefs we strongly encourage you to begin to apply the principles and concepts immediately. By doing so, your personal and professional leadership skills will advance dramatically.

Leaders develop effective leadership styles as they pass through a series of sequential and essential steps. The points to emphasize are the *sequential* and *essential* parts of the process. In our model, one must attain Mastery of Performance, progress through Mach One Followership, and then ultimately slide toward the Center Seat Leadership end of the followership/leadership continuum. This sequence is possible only if you are willing to work hard to heed the lessons you encounter along your journey.

This is not a "how to" book, but a "how to do it better" book. It's a book for those who take personal and business leadership as seriously as jet pilots view their aviation skills. By necessity, jet pilots have a life-or-death intensity about what they do. You'll be given the tools to approach their level of intensity, or even go beyond it if you so choose. The result will be your ability to do the extraordinary.

We're confident that you already have an understanding about what it means to master something. Most likely, you also have studied and contemplated the concepts of followership and leadership, as well as where you fall on the continuum that connects them. It's important to gain insight into when you should be on one side or the other, and for how long. It is your ability to recognize the fluid connection between Mastery of Performance, Mach One Followership, and Center Seat Leadership that will catapult your leadership effectiveness to an exponentially higher level.

In Chapter One, you are introduced to a few primary characters as they are about to begin the second half of pilot training, which entails learning to fly the supersonic T-38, nicknamed the White Rocket. Imagine the sea of anxious faces that Captain Neil Williamson looked out upon as he began his briefing to the new members of Tiger Flight. Those sitting before him are not there by accident. They've passed through one of the most intense and rigorous filtering processes in existence to earn the privilege of sitting in that briefing room. They envisioned a dream of becoming jet pilots, and then carved a path for that dream to become a reality. They took advantage of the opportunities that arose, but, more importantly, *they* were the ones who created the opportunities to begin with. Yet none of them is aware of the life and leadership lessons they are about to learn. Some lessons will be learned immediately; others will take decades to be fully revealed.

FINAL QUESTION

WHAT OPPORTUNITIES ARE YOU CURRENTLY CREATING FOR YOURSELF THAT HAVE THE POTENTIAL TO IMPROVE YOUR LEADERSHIP EFFECTIVENESS EXPONENTIALLY FOR YEARS TO COME?

2

1:00 A.M.

The alarm clock barely rang before Lieutenant Jack Logan reached over to turn it off. Even at 1:00 a.m., he wasn't one to hit the snooze button. Still, the several hours that had passed in sleep—four, maybe five at most—seemed to have flashed by in a wink. Sliding out of bed, he headed straight for the shower, thankful it would help him wake up. Standing a fit six feet and with dark hair, he was the grit and polish of which Air Force pilots were made, with a hint of admirable repose. He'd worked hard to get to this point.

After showering, Jack quickly grabbed the flight suit off the chair in the corner where he'd intentionally placed it the night before. Slipping it on, he mentally reviewed the day that stretched before him.

He made his way to the kitchen and flipped the switch on the coffee pot without having to think about it; as usual, the grounds and water were primed the night before. In the flurry of the morning routine, coffee reminded Jack of home. His parents' Midwestern suburban household ran like clockwork. His mother always brewed coffee before daylight to help set the working-class family in motion. The Logans moved through their lives with a methodic joy, one foot in front of the other and no step miscalculated. Jack took that discipline to heart before he was even old enough to peer over the counter; it served him well as he moved tirelessly through one challenge after another. He worked full-time to attend a state college and earn his pilot's license. Then he graduated from Officer Training School, the three-month course that led to his commission as a second lieutenant. Through it all, he maneuvered like a man with a checklist and a mission, in true pilot form.

After pouring some creamer, Jack quizzed himself on one of the many Boldface procedures stuck to the refrigerator by magnets. He knew he could be called upon during the morning stand-up "what if" scenarios, or during flight briefings, and debriefings, to recite, verbatim, these specific Boldface emergency procedures.

Anticipating the long day ahead, Jack sat at the tiny kitchen table and began his morning ritual of "Chair Flying"—a realistic simulation of normal and emergency procedures. The goal was to learn every procedure until it became a habit. He began by putting on his flight gloves. Then he put on his flight helmet, clicked the oxygen mask into place, and lowered the visor. Placing his right hand on an imaginary control stick and left hand where the throttles would be located, he looked down at the checklist attached with Velcro to his thigh and began to "fly" from his kitchen table tarmac.

He began with the Engine Start Procedure; one misstep or delay could cost tens of thousands of dollars in engine damage in the real airplane. In a matter of days, he would be in the White Rocket, spinning its engines for the first time. Heaven help him if an engine overheated or suffered some other preventable malfunction during the start procedure. From the comfort of his kitchen table he practiced giving each hand signal of the start sequence. Then he methodically proceeded through every step of the Engine Start Procedure, touching each imaginary switch, button, and control. He practiced every malfunction in the book and rehearsed the motions he would do in the actual jet trying to make everything a habit so that, in the heat of a real emergency, he wouldn't have to think. Instead, he would react without delay. Chair Flying was the time-honored method used by thousands of pilots before him, so he accepted it without question.

Before Jack knew it, it was after 2:00 a.m.; time to leave his imaginary cockpit and finish getting ready for the drive to base. He brushed his teeth and shaved while memorizing additional material. He reviewed the Limitations—numerical limits and airplane-performance parameters that had to be memorized cold—that were taped to his mirror on small pieces of paper. He returned to his room to grab his hat, keys, and wallet. It was part of his routine. He walked around the room, choosing to look at three of the multiple schematics, or diagrams, that lined the walls at eye level—everything from the hydraulic system to the electrical system to the brake system. He spent five minutes reviewing each one before leaving.

Finally ready to start his day, Jack poured one last cup of coffee into his travel mug, and headed out to the car to make it to the base by 3:00 a.m. Arriving at the squadron, he entered the flight room where the rest of Tiger Flight trickled in, well in advance of scheduled report time.

"Mornin', Jack!" Lieutenant Dewey Clark ("Mace") said as Jack entered the room. "Get any studying in yet today?" It was a rhetorical question they all understood. Mace smiled broadly, obviously enjoying his reference to a good 3:00 a.m. joke.

"I don't know how you do it as a married guy." Jack admired Mace's focus and determination. Married UPT students were a minority. The rigors of the program wreaked havoc on most marriages, but Jack figured if anyone could make it work, it would be the levelheaded, upbeat, hardworking Mace. He and his wife had met in college, where he was an aeronautical-engineering major and an ROTC cadet. He was the type who could persevere through anything with a mix of common sense and sheer determination.

Mace almost hadn't made it into UPT. Flying small fighter-type jets and trainers is one occupation in which height can work against you, since there's only so much room in a cockpit. There are strict sitting-height limitations for pilots who fly jets with ejection seats, given the minimal space between a pilot's helmet and the canopy. Mace had measured just under the maximum limit. Before entering UPT, he was sure he would be labeled with a nickname related to his height. He also knew that other nicknames came from a major screwup that a fellow pilot witnessed. It was, however, his qualities as a "nice guy" that earned him the moniker of "Mace."

One morning, he came into class at the beginning of UPT with red and swollen eyes. He told how, the night before, he had pulled into the parking lot of his apartment complex and watched a woman he believed to be his wife's friend struggling to load a large box into the back of a van. He parked as she went around to the front, presumably to get her purse. As he picked up a box intending to help her load it, she, not realizing who he was, became startled and sprayed him with a small container of Mace that was attached to her keychain. He dropped the box, breaking every piece of antique china inside. His flight mates quickly began calling him "Mace."

In his thick Boston accent, Preston Chatsworth III picked up where Jack had left off, but with distinctly less polish. "Mace, you might consider making a decision between your wife and your wings," he said. "I don't think you're gonna have both at the end of training. I've seen your wife, and I'd definitely choose her over the wings." After knowing the guy for months now, Jack recognized that Chatsworth wasn't *intentionally* offensive. He was just making another poor attempt to create group camaraderie with a little humor. Chatsworth was the guy in class who never studied quite as hard as others, but always seemed to have the answers and perform well under pressure. In spite of all this, he was well liked by his flight mates, though they found it hard not to make fun of him—Chatsworth had made a point of letting them know early on that he was "Preston Chatsworth . . . *the Third*." Lieutenant Carley Macfadden couldn't resist calling him "The Tenth" in a friendly effort to make fun of how seriously he took himself. While initially irritated by a handle that he knew was poking fun at him, Chatsworth eventually started wearing it as a badge of honor, even referring to himself as "The Tenth."

"Hello, Lieutenant," Carley said.

"Mornin', Dublin," Jack said, throwing his hand up in the air for a high five. Already, Carley had been branded with a nickname that referred not only to her Irish heritage, but also to her ability to out-drink the men of Tiger Flight. It's been said that in Dublin, 9800 pints are enjoyed every hour from the five o'clock work whistle on Friday afternoon until the following Monday. As her classmates soon learned, this striking lass was just as capable of tossing back ale as any Dubliner. She was also a solid member of Tiger Flight. She had worked in the business world for two years after college before entering UPT, and was known and admired for her common sense and ability to outperform most of her male counterparts.

As Dublin took her seat next to Jack, in ran Gerry Barrett, who was always pushing the limit. He arrived just in time. "T-Bird in the house," he said as he slapped Jack and Mace on the back and grabbed a seat.

"T-Bird better keep a more careful eye on his watch if he wants to be a Thunderbird pilot. I thought you actually had to know how to tell time to graduate from the Air Force Academy as a Distinguished Graduate," Mace joked. He good-naturedly punched T-Bird and instigated a series of back-and-forth jabs.

Everyone knew that Gerry's dream assignment was to be a Thunderbird pilot, a member of the elite Air Force jet demonstration team. During a cross-country trip to Nellis Air Force Base in Nevada, home of the Thunderbirds, he and some of his fellow flight mates were hanging out in the Officer's Club—the O'Club, as it was usually called—one evening. Even though they were still in Tweets, Gerry had felt like a hotshot and maneuvered his way into a conversation with a beautiful brunette who sat at the bar alone enjoying a drink.

"He talks as smooth as he flies," The Tenth had joked to their group of friends.

"I don't think your buddy's gonna talk his way out of this one," a voice commented from behind them. The group turned to see a pilot in a Thunderbird flight suit. "That's my buddy's wife he's talking to. "And *that*"—he nodded toward the front door—"is my buddy."

The pilot walked through the door. If he'd been any taller or broader, he wouldn't have fit into the cockpit of his red-white-and-blue air-show jet. Before Gerry knew what was happening, his flight mates grabbed him by the arms and dragged him away.

"Nice goin', *T-Bird*," Mace had said, and Gerry's nickname was born.

Mace and T-Bird stopped their verbal jousting as Major Buford and his nine instructor pilots, or IPs, entered the Tiger Flight room from the adjoining office. The students sprang to attention.

"Take your seats," said Major Buford, a former fighter pilot. For the past year, he'd been a UPT flight commander. He had ruffled a few feathers of the higher-ups. Yet he was such an outstanding pilot and natural leader that his boss, the squadron commander in charge of all ten training sections, or flights, in the T-38 squadron, gave him plenty of leeway to do what he needed to do. Buford looked like a stereotypical no-neck NFL lineman. His tone and presence barreled over any distractions in the room.

"You've been on the flight line a couple of weeks now and some of you have already had your first flight in the White Rocket. You've been here long enough for me to see what you've got. Unfortunately, what I'm seeing is that you ain't got enough of what it takes," Major Buford said. "These morning stand-ups are your opportunity to demonstrate what you're capable of. This is the most intense preparation you can do outside the cockpit. As of today, the free pass that some of you apparently thought you had is being thrown out the window. I have instructed Captain Chandler, your flight standards IP, to give no breaks during morning stand-up. If you stand up and screw up, you'll sit for the day. Got it?"

An anxious silence took control of the room. No one wanted to be called on next. An IP leaned back in his chair, and the squeak of the unoiled springs sounded like the opening bell of a major fight about to take place.

Major Buford turned to the IP standing next to him. "Captain Chandler, the podium is yours."

Jack had heard that Captain Chandler was a rock of an IP—dependable, accomplished, with a commanding presence—who genuinely enjoyed teaching students how to fly the White Rocket. Nevertheless, when he stepped up to the front of the room, the heat was on.

"Okay," he began. "Here's your scenario. You're flying solo and experience an engine loss due to bird ingestion. You handle that emergency just fine and shut down the engine per the checklist. Your twin-engine jet is now a single-engine jet—and you know that if you lose your remaining engine, your only option is to eject. As you arrive back at base and are on final approach to the runway, you set up to do a single-engine landing. On short final, when you are just about ready to touch down, the controller tells you to discontinue the approach—to go around. Lieutenant Macfadden, what do you do?"

After a few seconds of silence, Dublin responded,

"THROTTLE(S)—TO MAX."

"Have a seat, Lieutenant Macfadden," said Captain Chandler. As Dublin took her seat, Jack glanced to the back of the room where the scheduler sat. Dublin's name was being turned upside down. The tension level in the room ratcheted higher. To see one of the sharpest students in the class mess up the Boldface put everyone else under considerably more pressure.

Captain Chandler immediately called on the next student. "Lieutenant Chatsworth, pick up where Lieutenant Macfadden left off."

With his usual air of confidence, The Tenth recited the Boldface:

"THROTTLE(S)—MAX,

FLAPS—60%,

AIRSPEED—FINAL APPROACH SPEED MINIMUM."

"Have a seat, Lieutenant Chatsworth," replied Captain Chandler, still looking straight ahead. Two of the top students had choked under pressure. The Tiger Flight room grew eerily quiet as the scheduler flipped over another magnetic nameplate on the scheduling board. The ticking of the round clock on the wall behind the podium was the only sound that Jack could hear.

"Lieutenant Logan," Chandler said, breaking the silence. "Can you enlighten us on this procedure?"

Jack was instantly on his feet.

"THROTTLE(S)—MAX,

FLAPS—60%,

AIRSPEED—*ATTAIN* FINAL APPROACH SPEED

MINIMUM."

"Well-done, Lieutenant Logan," Captain Chandler said as he stepped out from behind the podium. "Excellent preparation. Be seated." He looked around the flight room as Jack sat down.

"You all need to prepare as if your life depended on it. When I was in UPT, one of my classmates had to eject. The ejection wouldn't have been necessary had he been better prepared and performed his Boldface procedures correctly when it really counted—in the jet. He lost an engine about twenty miles from base due to an ingestion of birds. He handled the engine loss procedure perfectly, but when he arrived back at base, he was flying too fast and was too high to land as he approached the runway. He had to go around. Everything was fine until he had to perform the Boldface for a single-engine go-around procedure. He raised the flaps all the way up. I know you're new to the T-38, but it's no different from any other airplane you've flown with respect to the flaps. When you're low and slow, you'd better not retract them to zero or your jet will fall out of the sky. Unfortunately, that's just what he did. His jet started an uncontrolled descent to the ground and he had to eject."

"Gentlemen"—Captain Chandler paused, looking in Dublin's direction—"and lady. If you had to do a single-engine go-around on your next flight, would you be able to perform the Boldface correctly? Or would you end up giving the jet back to the taxpayers, and possibly ending your career—or your life?"

* * *

After twelve hours on the flight line, Jack's long day finally came to an end. He took a shower that was as therapeutic as ever, and prepared for an evening out. It was Friday night, after all, and that usually meant cutting loose a bit. All the students knew, though, that the pressure was never really off, and even nights like this turned into study sessions in one way or another.

As Jack walked into the local pizza hangout, he spotted Dublin, Mace, The Tenth, and T-Bird holding court around a pitcher of beer. The pizza wasn't half gone before T-Bird, the poster boy for Air Force pilots with charm to match his looks, stopped flirting with a waitress and fired off the first round of questions.

"What is the maximum allowable speed to fly with the gear extended?"

"That's an easy one—two hundred and forty knots," answered Jack.

T-Bird pressed on. "What's the maximum airspeed for the flaps at sixty percent?"

Mace responded, "Two hundred and twenty knots."

The Tenth turned to Dublin. "Bonus question: How do you convert knots to miles per hour?"

"That's an easy one—multiply nautical miles per hour by one point one five to get statute miles per hour, so a hundred nautical miles per hour—or knots—equals a hundred and fifteen miles per hour," Dublin answered without hesitation.

"Ding, ding, ding," replied T-Bird, acknowledging the correct answer.

The questioning became more intense, and they continued until they couldn't take it anymore. By the time the pizza was cold, they'd all been up for at least twenty hours. Jack stood and said, "All right! Who's up for some Chair Flying?"

The entire group groaned and started for the exit.

"Don't tell me you actually thought I was serious! Now that *is* scary," Jack said with a smile, catching up with his friends.

It took some effort for Jack to raise his arm to insert the key in the front door. He headed straight for his bedroom, kicked off his shoes, and collapsed on the bed. His mind tumbled vaguely through the plans for the next day . . . *oil change.* He had to get an oil change for the car. *I'll have to remember to transfer my 3x5 cards to my book bag . . . maximize any free time sitting there in the shop. And then I'll come back home and transfer some more info to the cards. Maintain Aircraft Control, Analyze the Situation, and Take Appropriate Action. . . .*

He looked over at the stack of books and manuals on his dresser. The pile stood at least two feet tall. He smiled faintly through squinting eyes, reminded himself that he was loving every minute of this, and fell asleep next to the flight suit he'd tossed on the bed.

CHAPTER TWO DEBRIEF

PREPARE

No man ever reached to excellence in any one art or profession without having passed through the slow and painful process of study and preparation.

HORACE, ROMAN PHILOSOPHER

Achieving mastery is an accomplishment that can remain with you forever. It can change the course of your life. We go one step further and call it Mastery of Performance, for it is in the performance, or demonstration of your mastery, that everything comes together. Mastery of Performance allows students in pilot training to fly solo in a supersonic jet mere weeks after their first flight. Yet this concept isn't limited to the world of aviation. Indeed, it is a concept that can be applied to other aspects of life and business with great success. So, what is true mastery?

We achieve mastery when we possess the full command of a skill that results in consistent, repeatable, and reliable excellent performances. In this context, we are using the word "performance" in a broad manner. A performance includes anything from conducting an incredibly successful business negotiation to excelling in an athletic event to nailing an interview for the job of a lifetime or taking a group in an organization to a level they never thought they could achieve. It does not mean achieving perfection. We have accumulated tens of thousands of hours flying jets, yet we have never flown the perfect flight. We have negotiated myriad multimillion-dollar business deals, yet the perfect negotiation remains elusive. Getting 100 percent of what you want all the time is not realistic. But developing the ability to be completely prepared, to be well practiced, and to perform flawlessly under pressure consistently, *is* realistic. This is what you can do by fully utilizing the PEER Performance Model.

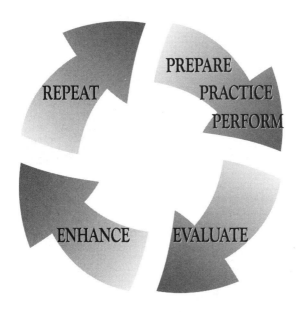

PEER PERFORMANCE MODEL

After decades of flying jets, we have articulated a performance model that we have successfully transferred to our non-aviation business endeavors—and to our lives, for that matter. The key to achieving Mastery of Performance is the PEER Performance Model. You can't do all of this alone. The acronym PEER is meant as a reminder of that. The individual elements are simple, but when combined they become powerful:

P—PREPARE, PRACTICE, PERFORM

E—EVALUATE

E—ENHANCE

R—REPEAT

This chapter debrief will focus on the first step of the model—
Prepare.

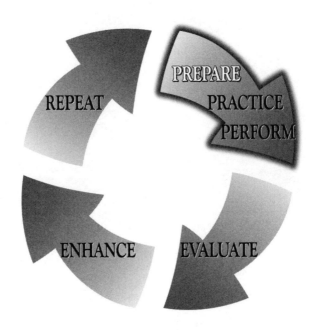

PEER PERFORMANCE MODEL

By reading this book, you have already opened the door to
understanding preparation in a way that you never before imagined. In
this model, there is no such thing as waiting until the last minute and
hoping that everything works out. Would you want to fly on an airliner
with pilots who weren't masters of preparation? Of course you wouldn't,

no more than you would want to undergo surgery with an unprepared surgeon. But stop and think for a moment why you *would* be willing to get on an airliner, putting your life in the hands of a pilot, or to lie down on an operating table, trusting your life to a surgeon. The answer is clear. You do these things because you are convinced that pilots and surgeons are fully prepared. And you may not realize it yet, but you are capable of preparing for what you do to the exact same degree.

Like the other steps of the PEER Performance Model, the Prepare step is multifaceted. Imagine a half-million pound commercial jet sitting at the end of the runway about to take off. A tremendous amount of energy, or takeoff thrust, is required to set that jet in motion and accelerate it down the runway to a speed that will allow it to become airborne. Much less power is required to sustain that jet in cruise flight. Just as takeoff thrust is what is needed to launch a jet into the air, Total Immersion is what is needed to launch the Prepare step of the PEER Performance model.

THE REQUIRED MINDSET: TOTAL IMMERSION

Total Immersion doesn't mean you have to sequester yourself from society until you emerge from the proverbial mountaintop as a master. Rather, it is the act of becoming and remaining focused, acting with intent, and removing distractions from the task at hand. Unrelated matters sit outside your bubble of concentration, and you never allow them to enter.

The way Jack Logan completely immerses himself in the Prepare step from 1:00 a.m. until he can do no more at the end of the day is a perfect illustration of this concept. The key to keep in mind is that this extreme level of commitment isn't something that you need to do for years on end. That is not reasonable to expect, and few among us would do it.

However, it is something that can be done for a limited amount of time depending on the skill that needs to be acquired. In Jack's case, it's around one year. In the case of an entrepreneur starting a small business, it might be more than that. But without this commitment, extraordinary results will be a lot harder to come by.

BRAIN PLASTICITY

The idea of "brain plasticity" in neuroscience bucks the conventional opinion that most brain development stops when we are young. Dr. John Medina, the director of the Brain Center for Applied Learning Research at Seattle Pacific University, writes in his book *Brain Rules*, "some regions of the adult brain stay as malleable as a baby's brain, so we can grow new connections, strengthen existing connections, and even create new neurons, allowing all of us to be lifelong learners."[1]

Our brains can "leapfrog" beyond our own former assumptions to give us new knowledge that is more valuable and more intuitive to our purposes. These new associations and connections make us more adept at our business—especially when decisions must be made quickly.

The more we prepare by Total Immersion, the more malleable our brains become. A flexible, adaptable decision maker who has reviewed a variety of potential scenarios is more likely to adjust to changing conditions with innovative, intuitive thinking than one who clings stubbornly to long-held ways of getting things done.

CHAIR FLYING

Chair Flying is repeatedly preparing until an act becomes second nature, and doing so in an environment that resembles, to the greatest extent possible, the real thing. It is the process of so ingraining the action, or procedure in your mind and body that you can perform with little thought and, if necessary, under extreme pressure. This is one of the characteristics that keeps pilots alive. Chair Flying trains pilots to think and act with complete clarity, even when their life is on the line. If you use the same techniques, you can become so competent in your chosen endeavor that you'll be much better able to handle any crisis that may arise.

Jack created a "cockpit environment" in his apartment. When he was Chair Flying, he wore his flight suit, helmet, and flight gloves. He strapped his checklist to his leg and exhaustively went through every procedure that he needed to make second nature. With enough imagination, you can create any environment that will serve your purpose. It's low-tech, but as effective as any preparation technique you'll ever use.

Perform every step the way pilots do when they are learning to fly a jet. As pilots, we never stopped Chair Flying, even after we had accumulated thousands of hours of flight time. When we transitioned out of the flying world and into the world of business, we brought Chair Flying with us. Instead of relentlessly preparing for flight procedures, we relentlessly prepared for negotiations, presentations, and the like.

One of our businesses routinely involves negotiating multimillion-dollar transactions. To prepare, we Chair Fly everything, from the meeting itself to the phone calls that set up the meeting. To Chair Fly an event, put yourself in an environment that resembles, as closely as possible, the actual venue in which it will take place. Whether the event you are preparing for will be in a small office or onstage in front of a thousand people, create a physical and mental environment that will help you most. Don't despair if you can't perfectly create the physical environment. Do the best you can. The mental aspect is what counts.

When it's time to do the real thing, you'll also be under more pressure. So, to the extent that it's possible, raise the pressure quotient by having others in attendance. And by *others*, we don't mean just your closest confidants. Bring in people who have a more critical eye than those who are your most loyal supporters.

Rick Davis is a world-recognized expert in communication and adult learning who has studied preparation extensively. He recently coauthored, with Dr. Stephen Stahl, what is sure to become the definitive book on communication and adult learning, *Best Practices For Medical Educators*. Davis is known for emphasizing that "it's all in the setup."[2] By *setup* he means preparation. He explains how extreme preparation results in more available "mental space" that can be devoted to being in the moment, as opposed to using that same mental space to concentrate on *what comes next*. Davis contends that such a level of preparation allows one to do something almost without thought, which is precisely the goal of Chair Flying.

ATP

Available Time Potential (ATP) is another highly effective technique in the Prepare step of the PEER Performance Model. It involves taking time that would otherwise be wasted and putting it to productive use. The key is to have reference material with you in a form that you can use. In this chapter, Jack hung up notes around his apartment. Whenever he brushed his teeth or opened his refrigerator, he reviewed information posted on his mirror and refrigerator door. For you, the solution may be anything from carrying 3 x 5 index cards to having a podcast or list on your preferred electronic device available whenever you have time to fill. No matter your circumstances, you likely have some time that can be converted to ATP. The next time you're in a waiting room or standing in a long line somewhere, see if you can create productive time. Come prepared. We guarantee that your productivity and bottom-line results will increase dramatically if you perform these steps with full intention and consistency.

Final Question

WHAT IS ONE THING THAT WOULD HAVE THE GREATEST IMPACT ON YOUR LIFE IF YOU PREPARED FOR IT USING THE PEER Performance Model TECHNIQUES OUTLINED IN THIS SECTION?

[1] John Medina, *Brain Rules: 12 Principles for Surviving and Thriving at Work, Home, and School*, Pear Press, 2008, p.271.

[2] Richard L. Davis and Dr. Stephen M. Stahl, *Best Practices for Medical Educators*, NEI Press, 2009, p.6.

3

"WHICH THROTTLE, LIEUTENANT?"

The tandem seating of the White Rocket, with student in the front cockpit and instructor in the back cockpit, was a departure from the side-by-side seating students were used to in Tweets. This also meant that student and instructor communicated through an intercom system, and listening to Jack's labored breathing through his headset grated on Captain Williamson. To him, Jack was yet another student pilot in a flight suit fumbling through cockpit setup procedures. Strapping into a T-38 for the first time was obviously monumental for anyone—and Neil was sure Jack was savoring every moment while congratulating himself for making it this far in the program. Flying with students on non-checkride flights was not something Neil particularly enjoyed, but it was something that check pilots were required to do on a regular basis. He actually *preferred* evaluating their progress on checkrides and then returning them to their regular IPs.

While waiting for a sign that his student was ready to begin, Neil recalled a joke he shared with some of the other IPs. Although he loved flying T-38s, he often said that at least in Tweets, with side-by-side seating, check pilots and IPs could reach over to grab and shake a student's oxygen hose in an attempt to ignite some dormant brain activity.

"Lieutenant Logan, let's try to pick up the pace a bit. I'm all ready to go back here," Neil barked over the aircraft intercom.

"Yes, sir, Captain Williamson."

Neil heard Jack adjusting his oxygen mask again and fought back the urge to clear his throat. He had guided countless students through the time-consuming process of learning how to perform T-38 checklists, and he wasn't thrilled at doing it yet another time. He knew, however, that few things they would learn would be as important. "Lieutenant Logan, I want you to understand the cadence and speed we expect from you when you run through these checklists, so verbalize every step. . . . Go ahead and start reading and I'll give the responses."

"Sir, should I start over, or should I continue from where I am?" Jack asked.

"Lieutenant, just continue from where you are . . . come on, this isn't any different from what you did for five months in Tweets, so let's get going."

"Okay, sir . . . Oxygen System."

"CHECK."

"Circuit Breakers."

"CHECK."

"Gear Door Switch."

"NORMAL."

"Flight Director Switch."

"ON."

"Aux Flap Switch."

"ON."

"Rudder Trim Knob."

"CENTERED."

"Throttles."

"OFF."

"Speed Brake Switch."

"OPEN."

"Compass Switch."

"MAG."

"Fuel Shutoff Switches."

"NORMAL."

"Landing Gear Alternate Release Handle."

"IN."

With the engines roaring and checklists complete, Jack took a deep breath as he taxied the sleek jet onto the runway and briefed Neil on the HAT check—the initial Heading, Altitude, and Turn Point. He pointed the needle nose of the T-38 straight down the runway and firewalled the throttles. Neil heard Jack strain as he held the brakes; he could only hope, but doubted, that his student was also scanning the engine instruments to ensure everything was working properly. He felt the brakes release and the throttles advance into full afterburner, forcing both of their heads back into the headrest portion of their ejection seats.

The jet leaped into the sky, accelerating rapidly; very shortly, it would exceed the maximum allowable speed to fly with the gear and flaps down. Neil was just about to bark a reminder, when Lieutenant Logan beat him to the punch. Unlike many students new to the T-38, Jack was able to retract the flaps and raise the gear before Neil had to intervene to prevent an overspeed. *Not bad*, Neil thought. But they had only just begun.

Sure enough, Neil instantly reined in his student. "Lieutenant, you're already a mile past the point where you were supposed to make a turn. Do you realize if we don't turn NOW we will fly right over a civilian airport that is directly in front of us?" When Jack did not respond, Neil guessed that he was glancing at the chart to determine which way he was supposed to turn. He had obviously forgotten the turn point he had briefed while rolling onto the runway a few moments before. In the next instant, the jet changed course as Jack initiated the turn.

Just as they rolled out on the proper heading, Neil heard a panicked "Oh . . ." through the headset. A bright red light lit up on each of their instrument panels.

Neil could hear Jack muttering under his breath: "Maintain Aircraft Control, Analyze the Situation, Take Appropriate Action." He was obviously aware of what that light indicated. "We have an Engine Fire indication on the number one engine."

Jack immediately recited the first step of the Boldface procedure for an engine fire:

"THROTTLE—IDLE."

"Which throttle, Lieutenant?!" Neil demanded.

"Uh . . . number one, sir."

Next came the second step of the Engine Fire Procedure:

"THROTTLE—OFF, IF FIRE LIGHT REMAINS ON."

A voice came over the radio. "Tiger 87, I see you are not staying on the departure course. Do you have a problem?"

"Continue to fly the plane, Lieutenant. I've got the radios," said Neil. "Roger, Tiger 87 is declaring an emergency. We have an engine fire and request radar vectors back to base for an immediate landing."

"Tiger 87, I copy your emergency. Turn right to heading zero-niner-zero and plan for a landing on Runway Two-Seven. When able, say fuel remaining, in minutes, and souls on board."

"Heading zero-niner-zero, Tiger 87 emergency," Neil repeated. Jack was approaching task saturation. Neil knew all the signs of someone who was at the point of not being able to process any new information.

"Lieutenant, what's your plan now?"

"I'm waiting to see if the fire light goes out," Jack said. "If it doesn't we'll have to . . . we'll have to . . . shut down the engine, sir."

If the fire light didn't extinguish after the throttle was placed to OFF, the next step in the procedure would require them to eject. But that was two steps ahead, and Jack obviously couldn't think that far in advance at the moment. Neil let thirty seconds pass, waiting impatiently for his student to say or do something. The fire light didn't go out. The procedure called for shutting down the engine.

"THROTTLE—OFF," Jack finally said out loud. "The left. It's the left engine," he continued, breathing hard and fast.

Neil agreed.

The controller's voice came through again. "Tiger 87, turn right to a heading of one-eight-zero degrees. You are cleared to intercept final for Runway Two-Seven. Emergency vehicles are standing by. State fuel remaining in minutes, and souls on board."

Neil jumped in. "Roger, one-eight-zero degrees heading, cleared to intercept final approach course for Runway Two-Seven. Two souls on board, standby on the fuel."

"Did he say one-eight-zero or one-niner-zero for the heading, sir?" Jack asked. "And tell the controller we have two thousand pounds of fuel on board, but I'm working on converting it to minutes of flight time remaining."

"YOU HAVE AN ENGINE ON FIRE! Forget what the controller is asking about the fuel. Fly the plane, and shut down the engine that's on fire!" Neil yelled.

"Yes, sir!" Jack replied.

Neil felt the decrease in power and knew instantly that Jack had shut down an engine. A brief scan of the instruments told him it was the wrong engine, leaving them with only one engine that happened to be—ON FIRE! Given their low altitude, only one option remained:

"Lieutenant, you just shut down the wrong engine! EJECT! EJECT!! EJECT!!!"

Neither spoke a word for several moments before Neil broke the silence. "If you screwed up that badly in a real jet, your career and maybe your life would be over right now." He paused and let that sink in. "Okay, we still have about thirty minutes remaining in this simulator session." They went through a few more normal and emergency procedures and completed the training mission.

Even though Neil was flying with a student assigned to Tiger Flight, he preferred to debrief training missions at his desk in Check Section, where he had ready access to his charts, diagrams, and training aids. Students didn't care for this much, though, as they were used to being in Check Section only to take a checkride—an intimidating, high-stakes event.

Neil let Jack sit in silence for a few moments to process his thoughts about the flight before he began the debrief. In the interim, he had gone to a vending machine to pick up two cans of soda.

Handing Jack one of the sodas as he returned to his desk, Neil began, "This was your first T-38 simulator period, and it's a lot to absorb coming from the slow and forgiving T-37. You let a few basic things really detract from your flying. The distraction of the engine fire caused you to become task saturated, and that led to your making a fatal mistake—shutting down the wrong engine. You could have lost your life, or killed someone on the ground, since you ejected with no idea of where your jet would come down. I'm sure it quickly became clear to you that things happen a whole lot faster in the White Rocket than they do in the Tweet." Neil leaned back in his squeaking chair and opened his can of soda. "Since this is your first simulator debrief, I'm gonna concentrate more on the mental aspects of flying than anything else; that's what got the best of you on this sortie. The philosophy of handling any emergency procedure will be the same for this and any other airplane you'll ever fly."

Neil paused to allow the gravity of that fact to sink in. In the quiet room, he noticed Jack's leg bobbing up and down. He despised such signs of anxiety, and stared at Jack until he returned his glance. Jack cleared his throat, and Neil continued. "What are the three steps to handling any emergency procedure?"

Jack began to answer, but Neil shut him down. "That's right. *Maintain Aircraft Control, Analyze the Situation,* and *Take Appropriate Action.* They aren't new concepts; I assume you've been using them for the past five months in Tweets. They will always be the foundation of handling any emergency procedure. I heard you mumbling the steps to yourself, but you didn't follow through. Keeping this simple formula in mind—and being able to act on it—will help you handle any situation and keep you alive." He gave Jack a condescending look that said, *Do you understand what I'm telling you?*

"Yes, sir, Captain Williamson."

"In terms of priorities, as you're flying around with an engine on fire, do you really think calculating your fuel-remaining in minutes was more important than dealing with the fire?"

"No, sir, I lost Situational Awareness."

"You can correctly analyze any problem and take the appropriate action. But if you forget step one—Maintain Aircraft Control—you could end up correctly handling an emergency, with all the switches perfectly positioned, only to career into the side of a mountain at five hundred miles an hour. Or, you might end up shutting down your only good engine, because you failed to maintain your Situational Awareness . . . which is exactly what you did."

"Yes, sir," Jack answered with a nod, sitting perfectly erect.

"Okay, let's look at the bigger picture of losing Situational Awareness." The words *bigger picture* grated on Neil as they left his mouth. Captain Brian Davis, one of the T-38 IPs who had recently been promoted to Check Section, used that term a lot. Neil—to his own chagrin—had inadvertently picked up the phrase. He shook the thought quickly. "Losing SA is obviously what got the best of you . . . and it happened immediately after takeoff, when you missed your turn. That, combined with the speeds the T-38 flies, resulted in your veering miles off course, just by a short delay in making the turn. Had this been a real sortie in the actual airplane, your IP would have had to take control of the aircraft, or air traffic control would have jumped all over you on the radio."

Jack's expression communicated that he understood and was in full agreement.

"Some might say that losing SA is pretty much expected on the first simulator ride," Neil went on, "but not me. You flew the T-37 for five months and passed all your checkrides. You should be able to make the first turn after takeoff at the right place, whether it's your first simulator mission or not." He paused, taking a long drink of his soda. "If you don't have the departure routing clear in your head before takeoff, you're bound to screw it up every time. Mentally staying just one step ahead of the jet is not enough. That would be like getting in your car to drive to base, a base you've never been to before, but thinking only about the turn out of your driveway instead of the entire trip to the base. You need to think *more* than one step ahead of the jet. The faster the jet, the more steps ahead you'll have to be. You know what I'm going to tell you is the key to all of this—don't you, Lieutenant?"

"Chair Flying," Jack responded. He was trying his best to absorb everything Neil was throwing at him.

"Exactly. I've seen enough students go through this program, and I can tell you that the ones who Chair Fly the most come out on top. Another key is to make your Chair Flying as realistic as possible. Even if you're at home, put on your flight suit and helmet, and strap a checklist to your leg just as you do when you're in the jet. Go through every procedure and maneuver until you can't stand it anymore—and then do it again."

A somewhat bewildered look crossed Jack's face. Neil knew that he was probably following these steps already, but his performance was an indication that he wasn't doing it enough.

"And another thing—use every spare moment you have to stay in the game mentally. Whenever you're sitting in some waiting room, driving to base, or getting a haircut, go through things in your mind. You'd be amazed at how much you can do this, even with a twelve-hour workday. There are plenty of opportunities—take advantage of them."

Neil caught himself sounding too encouraging for his own taste and snapped back into his typical tone. "The point is, Lieutenant, if you don't get your act together fast, you might want to reconsider what you're doing here." He then got up, crushed his empty can, and tossed it dead center into a trash container halfway across the room.

Rounding the desk and heading toward the door without looking at Lieutenant Jack Logan, he added, "Overall, not bad. Just think about what I told you, and Chair Fly more."

CHAPTER THREE DEBRIEF

PRACTICE

Practice doesn't make perfect, perfect practice makes perfect.

VINCENT THOMAS "VINCE" LOMBARDI, LEGENDARY FOOTBALL COACH

PEER PERFORMANCE MODEL

Smart Practice

Pilots attain and maintain their ability to make time-critical decisions through constant Practice, the second step of the PEER Performance Model. Whether through Chair Flying, simulator missions, or training flights, pilots spend thousands of hours sharpening their skills and dealing with scenarios they might encounter. Every conceivable scenario is practiced as they progress toward Mastery of Performance. You can do the same. In his book *Smart Talk for Achieving Your Potential*, Lou Tice wrote, "Deliberate preparation for a predetermined outcome results in high performance. You accomplish your goal hundreds of times in your mind (your simulator) before you try to do it."[1] Great achievers in virtually all fields—business, sports, the arts, teaching—attain their mastery not through gifts or abilities alone, but through constant practice. But does the *kind* of practice make a difference? It does. We call it Smart Practice— the discipline of practicing that which measurably moves you toward a predetermined goal. By the word *smart*, we mean useful. If your goal is to improve how you play golf, but you spend your time practicing hitting the ball with the handgrip instead of the club head, you will eventually become proficient at that, but you won't make progress toward your goal. This is clearly a lack of Smart Practice.

Task Saturation

We practice in order to become proficient at something. We engage in Smart Practice when we want to become *highly* proficient. The enemy of Smart Practice is Task Saturation. When we multitask at a high level, we simultaneously perform duties and absorb and process new information. We operate at our problem-solving peak. Yet, as Jack Logan's predicament in this chapter illustrates, when we succumb to Task Saturation, our body shuts down and we can no longer perform effectively. In the case of a pilot, this could result in loss of life. In the case of your business, it could result in shutting the doors or never getting your venture off the ground.

Task Saturation is the inability to process any new information as a result of being overloaded. This insidious, dangerous condition happens when you allow yourself to focus on fewer and fewer things, to the exclusion of all except one or two. The ensuing tunnel vision and inability to keep sight of the big picture can lead to dire consequences.

The following is summarized from reports issued by the Federal Aviation Administration and the National Transportation Safety Board (NTSB) that relate to a 1972 commercial airline accident.[2] While approaching Miami International Airport, the cockpit crew of Eastern Airlines Flight 401 noticed an unsafe Landing Gear Position indication. Even though the gear handle was down, the light for the nose gear was not illuminated. In accordance with procedures, the crew discontinued their approach to the airport so they could climb to a safe altitude and spend time diagnosing the malfunction.

The NTSB concluded that during the time the crew was determining the status of the nose gear, someone inadvertently bumped a control column. This resulted in the autopilot operating in a degraded mode in which it would no longer maintain the crew-selected altitude. Tragically, there was no aural or visual indication to alert the crew to this autopilot status change. As they labored to diagnose the gear problem, the aircraft began an almost imperceptibly slow descent into the Florida Everglades that resulted in the loss of more than 100 lives. The NTSB final accident report states that "preoccupation with a malfunction of the nose landing gear position indication system distracted the crew's attention from the instruments and allowed the descent to go unnoticed."[3] For our purposes, the operative word in this statement is "distracted." A succession of seemingly small but unusual events can quickly result in Task Saturation, at which point the most important objective is to regain Situational Awareness. We don't know exactly what happened in that cockpit on a moonless night decades ago, but we do know that no one is immune from Task Saturation, even the most seasoned professionals.

Situational Awareness

When Task Saturation sets in, the immediate goal for every pilot, businessperson, entrepreneur, or organizational leader must be to regain a view of the big picture—what pilots call regaining SA, or Situational Awareness. To prevent Task Saturation we use Smart Practice. To overcome it and regain SA when Task Saturation started to occur in the cockpit, we used Standard Operating Procedures (SOPs) and checklists to make sure everything was done that needed to be done.

In our business life, we've also created SOPs and checklists. Following SOPs and referring to our business checklists has helped us maintain Situational Awareness. In one instance, we were on the verge of becoming Task Saturated when one of our businesses began to grow exponentially. We did not have the infrastructure to support the growth—or so we thought. When faced with serving many more clients than the previous year, we had to ask ourselves: "Can we really do this?" After we reviewed the checklists and procedures we had in place, we were confident that we could—and we did. In subsequent years, adhering strictly to these procedures, we produced more cash flow, acquired more clients, and spent less time doing it. This was possible only because of the systems mentioned previously that we put in place in the beginning stages of our venture.

Brian Buffini, the founder of one of the most successful business coaching organizations in the world, says, "Without working within a system in business, you're a loose cannon, affected by things you didn't plan for and can't control, damaging your chances for success."[4] Standard Operating Procedures and checklists will allow you to maintain Situational Awareness when your current activities begin to overwhelm you or when your business grows. Have you created checklists that will save you when you are being pulled in all directions by deadlines, employees, bosses, and even your family? If you haven't, now is a great time to begin.

EQUITABLE TIME ALLOCATION

Equitable Time Allocation, or ETA, is another technique we have transferred from the cockpit to the business world to help maintain Situational Awareness. ETA is a way to manage an extreme amount of information that must be processed, by focusing for the minimum amount of time on specific items. When a non-pilot looks at the cockpit of a modern jet, it appears overwhelming, and that it would be impossible to monitor everything adequately. However, since pilots are trained to acquire information from one information source and then expeditiously move on to the next information source, any task can become manageable. Pilots know that they don't have to monitor everything all the time. Not even the greatest business leaders monitor everything all the time, and neither can you. However, you *can* develop a pattern of not allowing too much time to pass since you last looked at any particular item. That's how we monitored rows and rows of cockpit instruments. Try the same with your endeavors. Make a concerted effort to develop a written plan of action that lists all the things that need to be accomplished, and how often they need to be addressed. As you continue to refine your checklist, you'll be amazed at how your efficiency will increase. It will help you avoid the trap of Task Saturation, and it will ensure that nothing goes unmonitored for too long. In addition, when you experience your next inevitable crisis, reliance on the principle of ETA will ensure that you will be able to maintain Situational Awareness.

INTERDEPENDENCE

Smart Practice, Task Saturation, and Situational Awareness are inseparable. In flying, life, and business, the goal is to maintain Situational Awareness to the maximum extent possible. Smart Practice helps you avoid becoming Task Saturated and unable to deal with anything new that comes up by allowing most of what you do to become second nature. Likewise, you must have systems and procedures in place that ensure your enterprise will continue to thrive as you deal with the unexpected. Do this, and your chances of long-term success will never come into question.

FINAL QUESTION

DO YOU HAVE A PLAN IN PLACE THAT WILL HELP YOU MAINTAIN SITUATIONAL AWARENESS AT ALL TIMES AND AVOID THE INSIDIOUS TRAP OF TASK SATURATION?

---

[1] Lou Tice, *Smart Talk For Achieving Your Potential*, Pacific Institute Publishing, 1995, p.174.

[2] Source for details of accident: Federal Aviation Administration Web site, "Lessons Learned from Transport Airplane Accidents," http://accidents-ll.faa.gov.

[3] National Transportation Safety Board Report, NTSB-AAR-73-14-C-1, 12/29/72, p.23.

[4] Brian Buffini, *Oh By the Way . . .*, Olivemount Press, 2002, pp.40–41.

4

"I HAVE THE AIRCRAFT"

"We're six weeks into T-38s. I know you well enough to recognize when you're ticked about something," Jack said to T-Bird as they rounded the corner to the Life Support Unit to grab their parachutes, helmets, and G-suits.

"It's gotta be a hundred and twenty degrees out there . . . and Major Buford tells me this morning that students are supposed to park on the *outside* perimeter of the lot. There are all kinds of open spaces up front. You kiddin' me?"

Jack quickened his pace to keep up. "That's been the rule since day one, T-Bird. . . ."

"Show me where that's written, and I'll call it a rule."

Opening his locker, Jack tried to get a word in but was cut off.

"He's just jealous," T-Bird said with a sly grin, stepping into his G-suit and zipping up. "Major Buford's giving me a hard time because he knows that the ladies prefer my Corvette to his pickup truck."

Jack laughed as he grabbed his parachute. "You know it doesn't matter whether the rule's written or not. If you know about it, you'd better follow it. Until we've got wings on our chests, our opinions don't matter much. It's our job to follow, especially when it's your flight commander giving the orders!" He gave T-Bird a look that said, *Like it or not; those are the facts* and walked out the door to the jet. On his way out, he noticed Dublin at the other side of the room. He considered walking over for a quick chat, but saw that she was engaged in an intense conversation with another female student pilot.

Just then, Jack's IP, Captain Hinton, caught up with him. Jack immediately looked down and laughed under his breath at his IP's dusty boots, which had become something of a joke among the students. They all thought Hinton was a bit odd. He drove a motor scooter, carried a calculator everywhere he went, and always seemed immersed in paperwork. He reminded Jack of the stereotypical nerd from high school who always wanted to be cool but never quite pulled it off.

Jack was also aware of Captain Hinton's reputation around the squadron. The word was that he was on thin ice with his boss, Major Buford, because of two things. He had failed to pay a bill at the O'Club and he had recently engaged in a loud altercation with another IP in front of some Tiger Flight students. The discussion was about how Captain Hinton had failed to follow established procedures and almost caused a collision between two jets in the traffic pattern. The other IP made it clear that this was not the first time Hinton's flying skills had been called into question. Jack knew that one more incident could severely impact his position as an IP. But, being in a subordinate role, Jack put such knowledge out of his mind when he flew with Captain Hinton.

"Hey, Jack, I know we've already briefed our flight, but I think you've got aerobatics down. Let's tackle a loop and a split S, and then move right into stall recoveries so we can head back to base and beat up the runway practicing some touch-and-goes. I want you to nail your landings on your checkride."

Jack smiled. "You're the boss." He looked up at the last four numbers on the tail of the jet he would be flying: 1-9-5-2. *The year mom and dad were married.* He silently thanked them both for their support as he climbed up the ladder toward the cockpit.

* * *

Jack performed clearing turns to ensure that his assigned training area was clear of other traffic. Level at 15,000 feet, he added full power, lowered the nose, and accelerated like a bullet to attain the entry airspeed required for his first maneuver, a loop. Hitting 500 knots, he yanked back on the stick and was immediately shoved down into his seat, feeling as if not one, not two, not three, but four 300-pound wrestlers had just jumped onto his lap all at the same time. It literally took his breath away as he instantly reached six Gs. In the back of his mind, Jack knew that pulling the control stick so aggressively would warrant a comment during the debrief, but knowing he hadn't exceeded a parameter, he continued. Even as he was fully engaged in flying the jet, Jack imagined for a moment how the maneuver would look to someone sitting on a cloud next to him at 15,000 feet, watching his White Rocket fly through a 10,000-foot loop at 500 knots. Crazy.

Snapping back to reality, he completed the loop and returned, momentarily, to wings-level flight. In the next instant, he rolled the jet inverted and pulled back on the stick to initiate his next maneuver, a split S; essentially the second half of a loop. Clearing for possible stray student pilots flying below him, Jack continued to pull on the stick as his windscreen was filled with sky, then ground, and then sky again on his way back to the horizon.

"Nice job, Jack, nice job," remarked Captain Hinton.

"Thanks, boss."

Resisting the urge to peel off some more aileron rolls—spinning the wingtips like a drill through the sky—as he slowed down, Jack zoomed the jet up a few thousand feet, allowing the airspeed to bleed off. Slowing even more, he lowered the gear and flaps and then reduced to final approach speed. He initiated a stall, simulating a situation in which a pilot gets distracted and doesn't notice his airspeed is too low when in the landing configuration and close to the ground.

Jack recognized the first sign of a stall—airframe buffeting, shaking, and vibrating. He aggressively lowered the nose and added full power, performing a flawless recovery. Before moving to the next maneuver, he needed to clean up the aircraft, that is, raise the gear and flaps. Just as he raised the landing gear lever, however, Captain Hinton's voice came through his headset.

"I have the aircraft, Jack."

"Roger, you have the aircraft."

"I'm gonna demo a loop. Pay close attention to the rate that I pull back on the stick to get to six Gs. You were too abrupt on your entry."

Immediately adding full power, Captain Hinton lowered the nose of the jet to accelerate. As he passed through 300 knots, Jack noticed they were buffeting more than normal. His focus, though, was on looking outside to ensure no other aircraft were in the area before they began the loop.

"I can't believe it!" shouted Captain Hinton suddenly. In the same moment, Jack saw the throttles come to idle and the nose come way up to slow the jet. "Lieutenant, why didn't you tell me the flaps were still DOWN?!" Hinton screamed into the intercom, louder with each word.

Jack was flustered. "Sir, you took control of the jet. I assumed you were gonna raise 'em." He waited for a response . . . and none came. All he could do was endure the deafening silence and try to stay focused.

Captain Hinton had exceeded the maximum allowable speed permitted to fly with the flaps down by a huge margin, potentially causing structural damage to the aircraft. The passing seconds seemed like hours. Finally he spoke, but only to complete the Structural Damage checklist. The procedure called for slowing down and lowering the flaps to check for unusual movements of the aircraft that would indicate possible damage to the flaps. This procedure helped them determine if they could reasonably expect the jet to fly normally as they performed their approach and landing. Captain Hinton slowed the plane to approach speed and then down to touchdown speed—all was normal. They flew back to base expecting their landing to be uneventful, which it was.

Back on the ground, Captain Hinton was no less agitated. "Meet me in the flight room," he told Jack without even looking in his direction.

"Yes, sir," Jack replied, seeing Hinton reach for the aircraft logbook. Every flight required an entry, details of the flight itself—date, duration, as well as any unusual event that happened on a flight, so that maintenance could check it out before the aircraft could be cleared to fly again.

While walking down the hall, Jack met Mace. "How'd it go with the human calculator?" he asked.

"Tell ya' later," Jack said, raising his hand and cutting him off.

Jack hardly had the chance to sit down before Captain Hinton came through the door and headed straight for his chair at their Tiger Flight room briefing table. He wasted no time launching into the debrief.

"Lieutenant, the number one thing we're here to teach is the importance of exercising good judgment. Yes, we have procedures and checklists for most situations, but it's not possible to write a checklist for absolutely everything that can happen in an aircraft. That's where judgment comes in . . . and that's what you are here to develop." He paused. Jack looked straight at him, still not understanding what he had done wrong, but starting to consider the possible consequences.

"When I took control of the jet today to demonstrate a loop," Hinton continued, "you should have told me the flaps were still down. Your judgment was severely lacking."

"I had no idea what your plan was. I didn't realize that you—"

"By this stage in the program you should have grasped the importance of speaking up if you saw something wrong. As we accelerated and were about to overspeed the flaps, why didn't you open your mouth?"

Jack was taken aback. "Respectfully, sir, as we were accelerating, the jet was really buffeting and shaking. . . ."

"Lieutenant, I didn't ask for your input and I don't want it. This debrief is over." Hinton was done and gone.

Jack found an empty flight room down the hall, bought a bottle of water from the vending machine, and spent the next twenty minutes trying to debrief the flight for himself, playing out the scenario in his head time and again. While everything he had learned up to this point told him he had handled the situation properly, he still wrestled with more questions than answers. His earlier conversation with T-Bird passed through his mind. *Follow orders . . . do what needs to be done.* How could words that had seemed so clear just hours before seem so ambiguous now?

* * *

"That's ridiculous! There's no way you could have been expected to know how to respond in that situation," T-Bird said, grabbing another slice of pepperoni pizza as he joined up with some of his flight mates in a local pub at the end of a long day. "Mind reading is not a required skill of student pilots. The guy's some kind of high-strung geek living in a world of facts, figures, and formulas instead of people."

"As an IP, he deserves a certain amount of respect," Dublin said as she looked up to see The Tenth coming through the door.

T-Bird moved close to her face. He smiled mischievously. "Should I respect you?"

Dublin stepped even closer. She looked at his mouth as though she were going to kiss him and then whispered, "I've seen the women you go out with. I don't think you could handle a woman you respected."

She smiled broadly at him and stepped away, leaving him panting playfully.

Just then Jack joined the conversation. "Dublin, when I saw you in the Life Support Unit today, it looked like you were involved in quite a conversation with one of your fellow female pilots. I don't think I've seen her around before."

"I guess it did get a bit heated. She's actually someone I knew from college. She's in the class behind us, so she's brand new to the T-38 squadron. Anyway, she was making a big deal about an off-color joke that some IP told in her flight and my point to her was to get over it," Dublin said.

"Based on the body language I saw, she didn't exactly seem to agree with what you were telling her," Jack responded.

"You're right. She didn't," Dublin replied. "She thought she needed to defend the female gender because someone had the poor taste to tell an inappropriate joke. I told her I thought her response was way out of proportion. There are things to fall on your sword about, but that isn't one of them."

"I admit, I can't even begin to understand the extra hassles women have to deal with in UPT. For what it's worth, you really seem to focus on what's important. It's pretty impressive that you wouldn't let anything like that knock you off course," Jack replied.

Dublin was about to respond, when The Tenth approached them.

"Looks like I missed something good," The Tenth said, taking a seat. "At least the pizza's still warm." He folded a slice in half lengthwise and took a big bite but stopped mid-chew, looking at the others. "What's going on?"

Dublin spoke up. "Jack took some heat on a flight today."

"We had a flap-overspeed," Jack explained. "I've been trying to figure out what happened."

"What's to figure out?" T-Bird filled in The Tenth. "He was transitioning between two different maneuvers, Captain Hinton took control of the jet, failed to check the configuration, didn't notice the flaps were still extended, and over-sped the flaps. End of story."

"Jack, don't sweat it, it's not like you busted a checkride," The Tenth said as he walked to the counter to order a beer and then pulled T-Bird away to play darts.

Dublin and Jack sat alone. "So . . . do you really feel like you did something wrong?"

Jack paused. "Thinking back to those moments in the jet, no way. Hinton took control, and I was just a passenger after that. If I had more experience, or could think further ahead of the airplane, I would have thought to say something. But that was the first time my IP took over before I cleaned up the jet."

"Which is why it's not your fault!" T-Bird shouted.

Jack shot him a look that told him to go back to his dart game. He turned to Dublin. "What confuses me is that Captain Hinton was out of control. But maybe he had a point that I'm not seeing."

"If he did, what would it be?" Dublin asked.

Jack sat up straight for the first time all evening. "Well, even though we all know that Hinton should have made sure that the flaps were up, he kept insisting that *I* had used poor judgment. Maybe he's right. What I should have been able to do was tell him that the flaps were still down."

Dublin smiled. "I'm impressed, Jack—attitude *and* perspective."

"Don't get me wrong; I still think I'm right," said Jack with a bit of a laugh. "I just figure I'd better try to find the lesson that might be buried somewhere in his reaction."

CHAPTER FOUR DEBRIEF

PERFORM

We are never more discontented with others than when we are discontented with ourselves.

HENRI FREDERIC AMIEL, NINETEENTH-CENTURY SWISS PHILOSOPHER

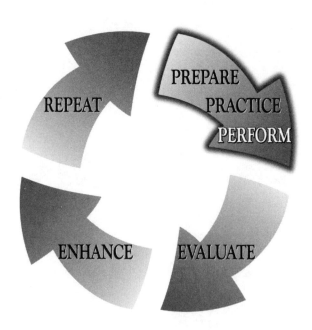

PEER PERFORMANCE MODEL

Whether you are overcoming pre-interview jitters for the job of a lifetime, presenting your business plan to investors, or leading a group within an organization, the outcome will be determined by the degree to which you are able to perform with confidence. A "performance" is any situation in which you demonstrate the results of your Prepare and Practice steps. If student pilots in their twenties can gain the confidence to fly a supersonic jet solo within weeks of their first flight, don't you think you can overcome whatever stands in your way to performing with confidence? You may be older than the student pilots in our story, so you likely have something even greater to draw upon that they do not yet possess—experience.

Yet how were they able to do the extraordinary without it?

Preparation and Smart Practice are the keys that open the door to performing with confidence. Pilots prepare with Total Immersion, and they engage in countless hours of Smart Practice to make every step second nature. When the two are combined, skill level grows exponentially and an unparalleled confidence results.

Picture this: two sisters who burst onto center court and change the way tennis is played; or a college dropout who has the confidence to create a start-up that would change the way the world uses computers.

You can picture these examples because they are real. But have you noticed these individuals are not unlike the student pilots in our story? They each have executed the Preparation and Practice step, and achieved the extraordinary even without having decades of experience.

The Williams sisters' courage, confidence, and athleticism changed the world of women's tennis forever. They racked up impressive victory after victory. Their accomplishments include Olympic gold medals, Grand Slam titles, and extended time atop world tennis rankings.

In our other example, imagine the confidence it took for the cofounder of Microsoft, Bill Gates, to drop out of Harvard and create a start-up. Indeed, he set out to create a business which a company as dominant as IBM did not envision. If Bill Gates hadn't had complete confidence in what he was doing, we never would have heard of Microsoft.

PERFECTING PERFORMANCE WITH FEEDBACK

Former New York City mayor Ed Koch was famous for soliciting feedback. He asked countless people through the years, "How am I doing?" He wanted to know how effective his policies were, and what he needed to do to improve his performance. In the same vein, pilots literally live or die based on feedback and how they process it.

There is perhaps no profession that operates more on the principle of feedback than aviation. Pilots receive feedback on virtually everything they do. In the cockpit, gauges, warning horns, and flashing lights provide instantaneous feedback on the behavior of the aircraft. Every input a pilot makes is recorded by Flight Data Recorders. Every radio call is recorded by air traffic control and every word a pilot utters in the cockpit is recorded by a Cockpit Voice Recorder. Following any incident, every fraction of a second is analyzed by accident investigators, and sometimes by attorneys and juries. All of this results in feedback in one form or another.

Feedback is available everywhere, yet in most instances, you'll have to work harder than a pilot to identify it. While much business feedback comes from metrics and market studies, it is the human element of feedback that really counts. No matter what business you're in, how you interact with people will always be a major factor in your long-term success.

Feedback is all around you, all the time. What you do with it can make a dramatic difference in your performance. Positive feedback reinforces or enhances our positions or actions. It encourages us and validates the effort we have invested into developing our ability to perform. What about negative feedback? While we can't control the negative feedback that we receive, we *can* control how we respond to it. The ability to deal with negative feedback effectively can be one of the most beneficial business and life skills that you ever develop.

In this chapter, Jack Logan made it his responsibility to find a way to deal with Captain Hinton's negative feedback and walk away with something positive, something that he could learn. Likewise, you are responsible for turning a subordinate's or superior's negative feedback into positive action. One tool you can use to do this is a RED Check.

RED Check for Negative Feedback

To address negative feedback in more detail, we offer the RED Check, featuring the steps we created as pilots and successfully transferred to our business endeavors:

Remove the Emotional Element: "Fighting fire with fire" doesn't work in negative feedback situations. Emotions do nothing more than fog the lens to what can be an enlightening view of the situation.

Evaluate and Find Value: When receiving negative feedback, make it a point to discover the morsel of value, no matter how small it may be.

Decide to Make Necessary Changes: This is the most important step—how to turn negative feedback into positive changes and actions. Regardless of what is learned, the final action step is what makes the difference.

APPLICATION: STRENGTHENING MASTERY OF PERFORMANCE

As noted, an important element of turning negative feedback into positive action is removing the emotional element. In Chapter Four, even though it wasn't his concern, T-Bird experienced an emotional reaction after he heard about what had transpired between Jack and Captain Hinton. Yet Jack was able to remove the emotional element. He took what appeared to be unfair and unwarranted feedback from Captain Hinton, analyzed it, and considered the changes he could make to improve his performance. This type of approach breeds Mastery of Performance, and should always be the takeaway when receiving negative feedback.

Are you processing all information—good or bad—from all of your "instruments"? If you receive information from an instrument—a board member, a competitor, a customer, a subordinate, a superior—are you recognizing the value in that flashing light, so to speak? Are you moving forward to make changes and build a stronger operation based on that information? Are you like Mayor Ed Koch and constantly asking those above you and below you, in one form or another, "How am I doing?"

When Mastery of Performance is your goal, no feedback is actually negative, because you will always turn the negative into something positive. Then feedback becomes, as Ken Blanchard noted, "the breakfast of champions."[1]

FINAL QUESTION

WILL YOU TAKE MAXIMUM ADVANTAGE OF THE RED CHECK THE NEXT TIME YOU FIND YOURSELF DEALING WITH NEGATIVE FEEDBACK?

[1] Ken Blanchard, Stephen Johnson, *The One Minute Manager*, HarperCollins, First Published in1981, p.67.

5

BLACK, WHITE, AND GRAY

The following Monday, Neil sat in his cubicle in Check Section. He had just returned from the vending machine with a bottle of water and bag of peanuts after debriefing a checkride. His day was coming to an end. Flipping through the latest issue of *Aviation Week* before he headed home, he couldn't help but hear Captain Brian Davis's voice rising from the next cubicle.

"... I'm sorry to say that I can't pass you on this checkride." The fact that Captain Davis was busting the student caught Neil's interest.

Captain Davis explained, "Most of your deviations were not major. They were minor, and you were obviously well prepared for the check. The fact remains, though, that you didn't perform up to standards of maintaining airspeed within acceptable parameters. On one approach you were fifteen knots fast and never corrected. On the next approach, you were slow and didn't correct quickly enough to get back within limits. And, as you recall, once you did add power to increase speed, you added too much power and didn't continue your descent to the runway, which resulted in having to discontinue the approach...."

Neil listened intently. *This guy needs to know the consequences of having to discontinue an approach and not being able to land—he could run out of gas if it happens at the end of a mission!*

". . . I don't want you to panic though. Based on your overall performance, I'm confident you'll do a great job on your re-check."

Neil was well aware of Davis's reputation for always finding some way to be positive and reassuring in his checkride debriefs, regardless of how the student had performed. Neil was hearing it in action. He closed his magazine.

"As you prepare for your re-check," Captain Davis was saying, "I want you to focus on one thing only . . . the *speed* of your crosscheck. You need to move your eyes more quickly as you go from one instrument to the next. The best way to practice this is to tape the cockpit diagram to your wall where you study. Simply move your eyes from instrument to instrument as rapidly as you can, at a speed that will allow you to process the information and move on to the next one. Repetition is the key . . . simple repetition."

Neil respected Captain Davis. In *his* mind though, a good debrief informed the students what they had done wrong and pounded home the point of what the consequences would be if they failed to correct it.

"Captain Davis, I know that, for some reason, I let my lack of airspeed control affect my performance today, but . . ." The student's voice trailed off.

Neil sat back, crossed his arms, and anticipated a typically lame excuse from the student. He was shocked when the student told Captain Davis, ". . . I actually learned a lot from flying with you. I know what I have to do to get ready for my re-check. Thanks, sir."

Had Neil heard *gratitude* from the student who had just busted a checkride? He was dumbfounded. He knew his typical tactics got measurable results: intimidate the students into doing better by letting them know what the consequences would be if they didn't rise to the occasion. *How absurd for Davis not to mention the potential consequences of busting a re-check! He talks as if failure weren't even a possibility.* Neil's head spun. *Is Davis putting his student in jeopardy by not terrifying him with the reality of the situation, or is he perhaps onto an approach that I've never considered?*

Neil remained at his desk as Captain Davis concluded the checkride debrief. After the student had left Check Section, Neil's curiosity seized him. He sauntered over and struck up a conversation.

"Brian, did I just hear that student *thank* you after you busted him?"

He flashed a subtle smile. "Well, I guess you did."

"Okay, I know we've talked about this before, but come on, what gives?"

Brian laughed. "Neil, I know we talked about the rigid standards that we're expected to uphold, but when I was a check pilot in my previous airplane, we had a lot of success with the big-picture approach, as long as the performance deviation wasn't severe and as long as we believed the pilot could progress with minimal additional training."

"Yeah, but you came from flying C-141s, didn't you?"

"That's right."

"Brian, that's my point. It's a different story in a large four-engine jet like that with a full crew. There's always someone there to back up the other guy. We don't have that luxury in the White Rocket," Neil said smugly.

"Neil, when we gave checkrides in that airplane, we had to make sure that each pilot could perform on his own. Something could always come up when one of the pilots was out of the cockpit, you know. Anyway, in my short time here in T-38 Check Section, I've simply used the same philosophy I did in C-141s. So far it's worked."

"And you know this for certain?"

"I've actually kept track of the students who had small deviations that I technically could have busted them for, but didn't. In every case, they did fine, both with the rest of the program and on their subsequent checkrides."

"Well, I haven't given those kinds of breaks, and I'm pretty sure the guys I busted remembered it and didn't want to go through that process again," Neil retorted.

"You're right. I'm sure they wouldn't want to go through something like that again, Neil."

Brian looked like he was going to say more, but stopped.

CHAPTER FIVE DEBRIEF

STANDARDS

Leaders get out in front and stay there by raising the standards by which they judge themselves—and by which they are willing to be judged.

FREDERICK W. SMITH, FOUNDER OF FEDEX

Aviators' lives are on the line every time they fly—so their ability to meet standards is vital. While most companies may not be engaged in such life-and-death matters, their decisions often put livelihoods and futures on the line.

Standards are not listed as a separate element of our PEER Performance Model, because they are the underlying foundation of each of the elements. In the Prepare step, we work to determine *what* the standards are. In the Practice step, we determine *how* we are going to meet them. We demonstrate our competence in the Perform step. In the Evaluate step, someone else determines if we meet or exceed the standards.

STANDARDS: EXCELLENCE AS THE MINIMUM

Excellence is the minimum acceptable level of performance in aviation. Is there any reason why the same can't be true for your business?

If you are an entrepreneur, can you accept anything less than excellence and expect to be successful? If you are a decision maker, will average performance take you, or your company, where you want to go? If you are a business leader, have you clearly defined what excellence means in your business? If you are an organizational leader, do your subordinates truly understand what is expected of them?

In aviation, standards determine if you live or die. In business, they determine if your company will thrive or perish. Standards can't be created just to fill a square. Standards help guide how you handle matters ranging from daily activities to the unexpected crisis. They are especially useful in emergency and high-stress situations.

THE THREE SIMPLE RULES OF STANDARDS

The minimum standard for leaders of any company that strives for success should be excellence. With excellence as the common denominator, we have identified three rules for standards. They must be:

1. Clear. In the non-aviation businesses with which we are involved, the number one issue with standards has always been clarity, or more specifically, the lack thereof. In aviation, standards are black and white, measured by instruments that define the meaning of the word *precision*. When standards are clear, there is rarely an issue. When they are not clearly defined, a problem will result every time. How do you make them clear? By writing them down and ensuring that they are reviewed, by everyone, at regular intervals.

2. Understood by Everyone. Writing down expected standards serves a valuable purpose. Ensuring that they are understood, however,

completes a circle. In this context, the circle encompasses everyone in the organization. No one can be left outside of the circle and expected to be a valuable contributor. If you are a business leader or business creator, you must ensure that all of your standards are understood. If you run a small operation, you can discuss your standards with employees at regular intervals, relying on the principle of repetition to get your message across. If the organization is larger in size, empower people at various levels to teach the standards. Remember that the best way to learn something is to teach it. If people at all levels are responsible for teaching others about organizational standards, everyone will benefit. It's that simple.

3. Equitably Enforced. Enforcement of standards is always a difficult subject. In the aviation world, we enforced standards strictly. In our other business ventures, our underlying operating tenet hasn't changed. People thirst for and appreciate clarity and equitable enforcement of standards. Just think of the last time standards were not equitably enforced in your organization and recall how you felt. It's safe to assume that you can vividly recall the strife and discord that resulted.

STANDARDS, SELF-AWARENESS, AND EXPERIENCE

The contrast presented by the styles of Neil Williamson and Brian Davis in Chapter Five lies not in their individual approaches, but in how much self-awareness each possesses. Neil clearly is lacking in this category. Determining the extent to which someone meets standards requires judgment and a tool kit, if you will, that contains a myriad of options. Unfortunately, Neil's tool kit contains only one tool—a hammer.

On the other hand, Brian's tool kit gives him many alternatives. He has gained self-awareness through experience and has developed the ability to look at the overall picture and choose the right tool for the right situation. He determines if it's in the best interest of the pilot, and the organization, to provide a second chance to prove competency. By so doing, he creates an inspirational environment. The point is that success lies not in your natural style, but in your ability to use the most effective style for a given situation.

The more self-awareness you possess, the better you understand how to enforce standards and inspire others at the same time. Increased self-awareness is the result of learning from experience, as opposed to experiencing a learning situation, only to forget it shortly thereafter.

STANDARDS AND FLEXIBILITY

Even though standards in aviation are perceived as rigid, there is plenty of room for flexibility and even creativity in certain situations. Essentially, the higher the level of competence, the greater the flexibility one is afforded. A great example of this is the Apollo space program.

Neil Armstrong landed the Apollo XI Lunar Module, the *Eagle*, in the Sea of Tranquility on July 20, 1969. It is clear to any observer that only the most by-the-book astronauts would be selected to be a part of the most complex and challenging space mission ever attempted. Yet, precisely because of the large number of unforeseeable events that could occur, flexibility was something that could make the difference between success and failure.

Astronauts and pilots develop such an extreme level of competence in dealing with "the known" that, as a result, they have a massive amount of available personal resources to deal effectively with the unknown or unexpected. Time, energy, and attention are examples of the resources that can be "freed up" to greatly increase one's ability to problem solve.

In a sense, astronauts and pilots have taken full advantage of the PEER Performance Model and thus attained an extreme level of competence.

In an authorized biography, Neil Armstrong provided some insight into his perspective on standards and flexibility by saying that, "… I would have been willing to use my commander's prerogative on the scene and overrule the mission rule if I thought that was the safest route."[1] Indeed, it was just that kind of flexibility that saved the mission and reserved his place in history forever as the first man to walk on the moon.

On that history-making day in 1969, as Armstrong guided the *Eagle* toward the lunar surface, he noticed something quite unexpected about the intended landing area—a large crater strewn with boulders. With very little fuel remaining, he was flexible enough to switch from computer to manual control, bypass the intended touchdown target and safely land beyond it. As his heart rate spiked to over 150 beats per minute he performed flawlessly under the most extreme pressure imaginable.[2] It could easily be argued that his flexibility saved the mission. This is a great illustration of how standards can be firm, yet still applied with flexibility. Keep this in mind when setting up or enforcing your standards and you'll be a lot better off than if you focus only on the rigid aspect of standards.

FINAL QUESTION

HAVE YOU REACHED A LEVEL OF COMPETENCE TO THE POINT OF BEING FULLY CAPABLE OF DEALING WITH THE UNEXPECTED THE NEXT TIME IT INEVITABLY ARISES?

[1] James R. Hansen, *First Man: The Life of Neil A. Armstrong*, Simon & Schuster Paperbacks, 2005, p.387.
[2] John Noble Wilford, "Voice From Moon: 'Eagle Has Landed,'" *New York Times*, July 21, 1969, p.1.

6

TWO WHITE STALLIONS

Neil searched for the shoeshine kit that circulated through Check Section. He scanned a few of the cubicles before running into his boss, the chief of Check Section, Major Herrera.

"This what you're looking for?" The Major handed him the kit.

"Thanks, boss . . ."

"You've got the cleanest boots . . . and the highest bust rate," he continued, referring to the number of students who had busted checkrides with Neil. "I got the monthly report, and you're at the top of the list again."

That was all Herrera said about it. As the chief of Check Section and a highly experienced pilot, he had solid credentials, and Neil knew it. The fact that he didn't expand on his comment about the high bust rate was enough to make Neil think about it. Neil was proud of his high standards, but he didn't particularly enjoy the reputation of being nearly impossible to pass checkrides with. His recent observations of Captain Brian Davis had opened his eyes to the possibility of another approach. It was ironic that he was about to give a formation checkride with Brian, whom he knew also had equally high standards, but the lowest bust rate in Check Section.

He heard Captain Davis join the two Tiger Flight students who had come to Check Section for a formation checkride. Jack and Mace walked toward Neil's cubicle. "Morning, Captain Davis," said Neil as the others approached him. "Lieutenants." He nodded to Jack and Mace.

After the brief greetings, everyone grabbed a chair. Neil wheeled his out of his cubicle and over to a large briefing area. "All right, let's get started. Lieutenant Logan and Lieutenant Clark, you are here today to take your formation checkride. Like the other checkrides you've flown, we'll start out with a ground evaluation, asking you some systems questions, Boldface procedures, Limitations, and a few 'what if' scenarios. If you make it through that, we'll go out to the jets and fly. Lieutenant Clark, you'll be flying with me; Lieutenant Logan, you'll fly with Captain Davis. We'll let you know what maneuvers we want you to perform. Lieutenant Clark, you'll start out flying in the lead position. Halfway through the flight, we'll switch so Lieutenant Logan can fly the lead position on the way back, and remain lead throughout the formation landing. Even though you'll each be flying with an instructor, when you're flying the lead aircraft, I want you to make all decisions that need to be made. Consider yourself the formation commander. You're responsible for everything unless we tell you otherwise. Any questions?"

"No, sir," they responded in unison.

"Okay, let's get going with the ground eval." Neil continued without wasting any time. "When flying formation, what's the most important thing you have to keep in mind?"

"Don't run into the other jet," answered Jack immediately.

"Well said," Brian interjected.

True to form, Neil began firing away with systems questions, for which Jack and Mace appeared fully prepared. Neil turned to Mace. "Lieutenant

Clark, what components are powered by the Utility Hydraulic System?"

"The flight controls, landing gear, nose wheel steering, speed brake, and the stability augmenter." Mace brimmed with confidence.

Again Neil turned back to Jack. "Lieutenant Logan, what portion of the electrical system powers the speed brake?"

"It's DC electrically controlled."

"And what happens if you lose DC electrical power with the speed brake extended, Lieutenant Clark?"

"DC dies, sir, so . . . it can't be retracted."

"And Lieutenant Logan, why would we need to be concerned about that?"

"Sir, if you happened to be low on fuel and a long way from base, your fuel burn would dramatically increase with the speed brake extended, and you might not be able to make it back for a landing before running out of fuel."

After thirty more minutes of ground evaluation, they were one step closer to flying. Mace, paired with Neil, would be flying lead initially, and custom dictated that the formation leader brief the flight. Neil was pleasantly surprised at the end of Mace's brief. He didn't need any prompting before thoroughly and flawlessly whizzing through all details, including scheduled engine start time, taxi and takeoff procedures, departure routing, planned maneuvers, the recovery route back to base, and, ultimately, the formation landing.

"Solid briefing," said Captain Davis. "And we all know, as the briefing goes, so goes the flight. Why don't you guys head down to the Life Support Unit, grab your parachutes, helmets, and G-suits, and we'll meet you down there in ten minutes."

* * *

Perched at the edge of the runway, the White Rockets were sitting side by side. It was time to perform. Jack glanced to the side of the runway and noticed a parked vehicle. He knew that when the afterburners of both jets kicked in, the coffee in the cup he saw the driver holding wouldn't need anything to stir its contents.

In a matter of seconds, crews in each jet efficiently ran through their Before Takeoff checks:

"Takeoff Data."

"REVIEWED."

"Battery Switch."

"CHECK ON."

"Canopy Defog, Cabin Temp."

"SET."

"Engine Anti-Ice."

"OFF."

"Parachute Arming Lanyard."

"ATTACHED."

"Cockpit Loose Items."

"SECURED."

"Helmet Visors."

"DOWN."

"Flight Control."

"CHECKED."

"Takeoff Trim Button."

"CHECKED."

"Canopy."

"CLOSED AND LOCKED."

"Tiger 85 Flight. Winds are calm. Cleared for takeoff," radioed the

Whiley Air Force Base tower controller. With that, Jack watched for the visual signals from Mace, who would take off first. Mace gave the circular spinning fingers motion, the command to run up the engines and verify that all instrument indications were within limits. Next, with a head nod he gave the signal that he was releasing brakes and Jack was to begin an eight-second countdown to his brake-release time. Mace released brakes and began his full-afterburner rocket ride down the runway. Jack delayed for the procedural eight seconds and selected full afterburner to begin his takeoff.

Following a smooth takeoff, Mace cleaned up his jet by raising the gear and the flaps and entered a shallow turn a half mile past the end of the runway. The pressure was on for Jack to join the lead aircraft. He had completed this maneuver many times, but now there were *two* check pilots watching his every move—Captain Davis from the cockpit behind him, and Captain Williamson in the other jet. Jack judged his airspeed and intercept angle relative to lead's jet perfectly. Before he knew it, he was locked in a perfect fingertip position—with a mere three feet of separation between the wingtip of his jet and Mace's. Jack knew he was nailing this part of the checkride, precisely matching lead's every move. In ten minutes, they traveled the nearly ninety miles to the practice area. With the sun veiled behind a light layer of clouds, there would be no glare with which to contend.

"Okay, Lieutenant Clark, I want you to lead your wingman through some turns using ninety degrees of bank. After one in each direction, direct him to pitch out and rejoin," instructed Captain Williamson.

"Yes, sir," Mace replied.

Focused on providing a stable platform for Jack, Mace smoothly rolled into a ninety-degree bank turn. Jack was bobbing and bouncing, over-controlling his aircraft, but he stabilized the jet during the second turn. From there, he was rock solid. Mace rolled out to a wings-level position, belly to the ground, setting up for a pitchout and rejoin.

Jack received the visual signal that a pitchout was coming. Within an instant, lead rolled to ninety degrees of bank, revealing the entire underside of the jet. That picture lasted only a brief moment, however. Separation between the two jets increased at an astonishing rate.

After a four count, Jack aggressively banked his jet so he could catch up and rejoin with Mace, whose aircraft was maintaining a constant turn rate and becoming a small dot on the horizon. Suddenly, the dot grew larger as the smaller circular path that Jack's jet was flying brought the two aircraft together. The arrival of his jet at a specified distance from Mace's was Jack's signal to reduce his power so his overtake speed would not be excessive. If he didn't, he could easily make the mistake of zooming past the lead aircraft, blowing the performance standards of this checkride.

As Jack's jet approached Mace's, the sun emerged from behind the veil of clouds, revealing itself at precisely the wrong moment and in precisely the wrong position. Now, at the most critical point of the rejoin, it was almost impossible for Jack to see the lead aircraft. He reduced both throttles to idle, extended full speed brakes, and used a steeper bank than normal to control his closure rate, but he started losing sight of lead as his bank angle increased; the sunlight blinded him. He was following proper procedures; however, the appearance of the sun right in his line of sight, as he looked at lead, was going to require a change of plans. Realizing this, Mace immediately made a command decision. "Tiger 85 lead is breaking out."

With that radio call, he must have pulled back on the stick, because his jet was no longer on a collision course with Jack's aircraft. They were now headed in different directions, each traveling more than 400 miles per hour, rapidly resulting in miles of separation between their aircraft.

Both instructors remained silent, obviously eager to see how the students, who had each actually followed proper procedure, would get the formation back together.

Jack remained composed and rolled out to a wings-level position, scanning the sky for lead. In an instant he saw a small dot on the horizon, which he identified as Mace's jet. Jack called out over the radio, "Tiger 85 dash two, this is lead. I have you in sight. Enter a left turn, maintain your current altitude, and I'll rejoin on you."

Mace responded, "Roger, I'm level at fifteen thousand feet and entering a left turn."

With that, Jack moved his throttles forward to the full-power position and made an aggressive move. He was quite a distance away, so he lit the afterburners for a few seconds, which allowed him to pick up a significant amount of speed in the blink of an eye. The small dot on the horizon started to grow rapidly, while remaining in the same position in the windshield. They were on track to join up expeditiously. At just the right moment, Jack slammed his throttles back to idle and extended his speed brake. He had judged his high rate of overtake very precisely and slid right into a fingertip position, three feet away from Mace's jet.

The remainder of the flight went well. The only thing left to accomplish was to fly the recovery back to base and perform a formation landing—two jets with nearly the fastest landing speeds of any aircraft in the world touching down on the same runway at the same time. For the recovery to base and subsequent formation landing, Mace assumed the wingman position and Jack flew lead.

"Whiley Tower, Tiger 85, flight of two, is with you ten miles out for a straight-in full-stop landing," radioed Jack as they arrived at the entry point for their approach to the runway.

"Roger, Tiger 85 Flight. Winds are one-eight-zero degrees at five knots, but we've had some gusts. So far, the peak gust was fifteen knots. You're cleared for a visual straight-in approach to Runway Two-Seven." Jack knew that both his and Mace's skill levels would be thoroughly tested now, because landing in this maximum allowable crosswind was challenging for any pilot, let alone students on a formation checkride.

"Tiger 85 Flight, cleared straight-in approach to Runway Two-Seven," Jack responded. As they slowed, he relied on standard hand signals for communication with his wingman. With the thumb-pointing-down signal, he gave the preparatory command to lower the gear. Continuing to the runway, he made a pronounced head nod, the signal to lower the gear. With that, the landing gear emerged from both jets, perfectly in sync. The runway was getting closer by the second, so Mace increased the three-foot spacing between their wingtips to ten feet in preparation for touchdown. With strong and erratic southerly winds, the situation changed continually. Maximum concentration and focus was required from each pilot in this formation. Jack was focused on providing a smooth platform for his wingman—not an easy task. He concentrated on remaining aligned with the runway, knowing when to begin the descent to the runway, making the required radio calls, and dealing with the added stress of having a check pilot in each jet monitor his every move.

Jack knew that Mace, on the other hand, had his own challenge. Mace's job was to make the hundreds of manipulations of the control stick, throttles, and rudder to maintain a perfect position in relation to lead. To top it off, procedure dictated that he didn't even get to look straight ahead at the runway until moments before touchdown. His total focus would involve staring at the lead aircraft and maintaining proper position. He would have only fractions of a second to adjust to prevailing wind conditions as he lowered the wheels of the jet to the runway.

Passing over the last check-in point, Jack notified the tower. "Tiger 85 Flight, we're three miles out, gear down for a full stop."

The tower responded, "Tiger 85 Flight, winds are currently steady one-eight-zero degrees at ten knots with occasional gusts to fifteen knots. Be advised though that they are changing directions rapidly. You are cleared to land on Runway Two-Seven."

"Cleared to land, Tiger 85 Flight," Jack said, as the winds buffeted both jets. The fifteen-knot crosswind meant that both jets were angling, or crabbing, into the wind to maintain a ground track aligned with the runway. Like cars skidding on ice, they were pointed in one direction, but traveling in another. Just before touchdown, Jack would have to transition and point his jet straight down the runway, manipulating the jet's flight controls to avoid being blown off course.

Regardless of how well Mace had flown up to that point, Neil's check pilot instincts came to the forefront and his hands began to hover around the throttles and control stick. Mace seemed to be getting a little unsettled as his excessive inputs were causing the jet to bob up and down. Neil waited for him to correct the problem, but was growing aggravated. *"Lieutenant!"* he snapped. "Get control of your aircraft!"

Within a few moments, Mace was once again locked in position, but the ever-shifting wind conditions forced him to fight to maintain focus while processing continually changing information—everything from how the aircraft felt to monitoring the radio calls, to dealing with the stress of a checkride. If they got through this checkride, both pilots would certainly have to wring the sweat out of their Nomex flight gloves.

Flying in the lead aircraft position, Jack was now at the correct point to begin final descent to the runway. He had reduced power slightly to allow his jet to fly down a stable glide path. The winds were still working hard to force the two jets apart; Mace would have to work even harder to maintain his position as wingman.

Neil's hands hovered a millimeter away from the controls. He knew that Captain Davis was doing the same in his jet. Neil was confident, though, that whether Captain Davis took the controls or let Jack handle the landing, Mace would be provided with a stable platform all the way to touchdown. As both jets crossed over the approach end of the runway, flying at approximately 160 knots, runway lineup looked good.

Jack and Mace continued to fight the winds. Just fifty feet before touchdown, a huge gust of wind rocked both jets. To counteract the incredible force, both pilots had to slam their control sticks to a lateral position as far as they could go and then instantaneously return to a center position. If they didn't, their jets would continue to descend toward the runway with a wingtip likely striking the asphalt before the landing gear did. Neil was a microsecond away from taking control of the jet, but he resisted the urge, allowing Mace to demonstrate the scope of his skills.

Both jets touched down almost simultaneously, and on their intended side of the runway. With the main wheels on the ground, both students followed normal aerobraking procedure and pulled back on the control stick to raise the needle nose of the T-38 into the air. The drag—the force of the wind against the belly of the jet—helped them slow to taxi speed. Despite conditions that would challenge even the most experienced pilots, they had brought their aircraft safely back to base.

Neil couldn't help but think that the jets looked like two massive white stallions raising their front legs into the air with victorious riders on their backs as they returned from battle. *Job well-done.*

CHAPTER SIX DEBRIEF

EVALUATE

No pressure, no diamonds.

THOMAS CARLYLE, ESSAYIST AND HISTORIAN

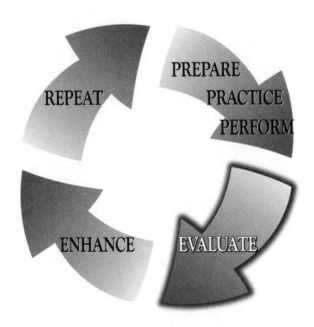

PEER PERFORMANCE MODEL

Lives depend upon the ability of pilots to fly and to perform flawlessly under pressure. While extreme preparation and practice provide the foundation for Mastery of Performance, evaluations measure the progress. They reveal strengths and weaknesses, and expose areas in which mastery has not yet been achieved. In the business world, evaluations are a way for decision makers to take the pulse of their organizations. For maximum effectiveness, evaluations must combine three key elements: Structure; an All-Encompassing approach; and High Stakes.

STRUCTURE

There are two vital elements of evaluation structure. First, the evaluators must be well qualified; second, the expectation of the evaluation must be clearly delineated.

If evaluators are not well qualified, those being evaluated will feel resentment toward them, distracting from the crucial task at hand. If you are in a leadership position, whatever you do, make certain those whom you select as evaluators have credibility. Otherwise, you will be wasting your time with the entire process.

Anyone subject to evaluations must know what skills and knowledge will be considered fair game on the evaluation. So long as they know that, the scene is set. Furthermore, there should be both scheduled and unscheduled—or, as we call them in the aviation world, *no-notice*—evaluations. During scheduled evaluations, specific skills are examined. During no-notice evaluations, everything is subject to being examined. Both types of evaluation structure are significant. The act of simply preparing for an evaluation is incredibly valuable to the person doing the preparing. It's not unusual for experienced aviators to spend weeks or even months preparing for an evaluation. Regardless of the outcome of the actual evaluation, the preparation and practice that preceded it are invaluable. Using a similar rationale, you should strongly consider having a no-notice evaluation program in place in your business enterprise or organization. Everyone involved benefits tremendously in the long run.

ALL-ENCOMPASSING

The second necessary element of effective evaluations is that they must, without exception, be all-encompassing. Businesses that use all-encompassing evaluations truly separate themselves from their competitors. The problem is that very few organizations do it. They cite costs, time required to conduct and review the evaluations, and other factors. Invariably, something breaks down in the operation and they can't pinpoint a cause that would likely have been exposed by an evaluation.

What does all-encompassing mean? It means testing for the vital, core skills, *as they are applied in various specific situations,* rather than testing for general competence in every conceivable skill—depth versus breadth. The skills must be directly related to successful mission accomplishment, whatever that may be for your business or organization.

For example, on an instrument checkride in a multimillion-dollar simulator, pilots must demonstrate the ability to perform a landing. They must be able to perform a normal landing in good weather. They must also land with an engine failure, with the loss of a hydraulic system, with a flap malfunction, under maximum crosswind conditions, with a landing gear malfunction, under adverse weather conditions, and so on. In the medical field, an equivalent evaluation might be to test emergency room physicians for their ability to diagnose a patient and prescribe the correct treatment. What's the core skill being examined? The physicians' ability to keep the patient alive. They must be able to perform under a variety of adverse conditions—a power outage, breakdown of a key diagnostic machine, minimal time with the patient, the onset of previously undetected symptoms. You get the idea: Core skills must be evaluated under a variety of circumstances.

High Stakes

The third key element of effective evaluations is high stakes. Evaluations with insignificant consequences are useless square-fillers. In the aviation world, a failed evaluation could result in unemployment for the pilot. Millions of dollars can be spent to train and qualify a pilot to fly state-of-the-art aircraft. In our story about pilot training, evaluations are a means to verify, every step of the way, that the investment on the part of American taxpayers is worthwhile. In business, evaluations are a vital tool to ensure that every dollar that is invested and spent is likewise worthwhile.

In non-aviation enterprises, it's not as common to see high stakes associated with an evaluation. But imagine how much better everyone would perform if high stakes were involved. Imagine risking the loss of your job if you were to fail a single evaluation. Would that motivate you to become fully committed to the PEER Performance Model?

Jack Welch, one of the most visible and praised CEOs in a generation, is known for instituting a program that identified the lowest 10 percent of scorers on company-wide evaluations and targeted them for termination.[1] These are high stakes. If you're an entrepreneur, you also know what high stakes are. Your evaluation might be the next presentation you give to potential investors. Not getting enough seed money for your venture may prevent it from ever becoming a reality. These are high stakes. Look at everything you do in the same light and there will be no limit to what you will be capable of achieving.

FINAL QUESTION

DO YOU HAVE AVIATION-STYLE EVALUATIONS IN PLACE IN YOUR BUSINESS OR ENTERPRISE?

[1] Jeffrey A. Krames, *The Jack Welch Lexicon of Leadership*, McGraw Hill, 2002, p.40.

7

"HOW DO YOU THINK IT WENT?"

After passing his formation checkride, Jack felt a tremendous sense of relief about having tackled and surmounted another huge hurdle in the pursuit of his wings. Entering a nearby empty flight room with Mace in tow, he approached the dry-erase board at the front of the room. He still wasn't used to the perspiration generated from wrestling a supersonic jet through a formation flight, let alone a formation checkride. He realized that both he and Mace almost looked as if they had just taken a dip in the O'Club swimming pool with their flight suits on.

"How do you think it went?" asked Mace as he took the liberty of settling into one of the cushy instructor chairs.

"For the first time on a checkride," said Jack, "we had not just one, but two check pilots watching our every move. That was pressure—from every angle, literally."

"And Williamson, of all people, was one of them!"

"Even though he was pretty rough on us during the ground eval, it seemed like he lightened up once we got in the air. Looking over at you guys, I didn't see him pounding on the instrument panel," Jack said with a chuckle.

"Actually he wasn't quite as bad as I thought he would be," Mace said. "I started to get task saturated when I was leading you through some of those steep turns. I wasn't too smooth on the controls and I knew it was grating on him, I could just feel it. . . . But he must have bitten his lip or something, because he didn't say a word about it."

Jack pondered the reason for Williamson's out-of-character response, or lack thereof. "Who would have expected that?!"

Mace nodded. "I was concentrating so much on being a stable platform for you to fly off of when I was leading you through the turns that I briefly lost track of the boundaries of our assigned training area. I felt that cold-chill panic for a moment—I think I even started literally to get tunnel vision. Somehow I got my SA back in time and prevented a bust, at least for that part of the checkride. Williamson was probably having a fit back there watching me, but he kept his cool. All he did was clear his throat a few times over the intercom."

"What else?"

"Well, I think we had Lady Luck riding with us on our formation approach and landing. I had a heck of a time hanging in there when we got below, say, a thousand feet on the approach. The winds were shifting around so much. It was all happening at the worst time, when we were being evaluated. What about you?"

"I don't think we just had Lady Luck with us, I think she brought along all of her sisters!" Jack said with a huge smile. "To be honest, a lot of the approach is a blur to me now, I know I wasn't exactly what you could call *stable* all the way down final approach."

"What happened about a mile out from touchdown?" Mace said.

"You mean when I decided to give you a look at the bottom of my airplane?" Jack asked with a sheepish grin.

Mace responded, "You put some instant separation between us and didn't let me know about it! When I tried to get back into position, I over-corrected and got a little erratic. That's when Williamson came a bit unglued."

"What'd he say?" Jack asked.

"He just sternly told me to get control of my airplane—and I did."

"You can use the wind for an excuse," Jack said.

"Well, I can tell you one thing. I can't believe how tough it was to deal with the winds," Mace said.

"The winds were in the weather forecast. We should have made a bigger deal about them in the briefing," Jack replied.

"I think we handled it okay. They didn't even mention it in the debrief," Mace said.

"I just need to make a lot more small corrections, especially when the weather is messing with us so close to the runway," Jack said.

"I'm with you on that one. But there's a bigger point," Mace said. "Williamson pointed out that no one can fly a perfect flight—ever, except him of course."

Jack laughed and continued. "I want to avoid being paralyzed by some screwup that I might make early in a flight."

"Yep, that's one of the biggest things we need to look out for," replied Mace.

Jack interjected, "When I made that huge altitude deviation on short final, for a second the thought of busting started to get me. I have no idea how I pushed through that one, but miraculously I did."

"I know what you mean. Sometimes I get bogged down by thinking that anytime we're up in the jet, we're potentially just seconds away from disaster," Mace said.

"I try not to think about that."

"Amen. Let's stop thinking about any of it and get outta here," Mace concluded.

"You got it. . . . Time to celebrate. First round's on me," Jack said, holding the door open and switching off the lights of the once-again empty flight room.

CHAPTER SEVEN DEBRIEF

ENHANCE AND REPEAT

A good athlete always mentally replays a competition over and over, even in victory, to see what might be done to improve the performance the next time.

FRANK SHORTER, OLYMPIC GOLD MEDALIST IN THE MARATHON

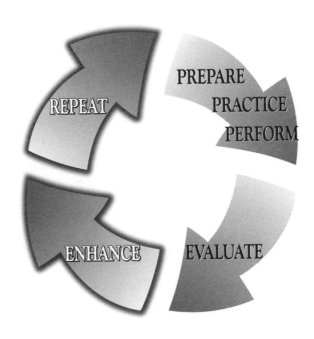

PEER PERFORMANCE MODEL

We have now reached the point where all the hard work that goes into the PEER Performance Model comes together. The question is, how do we enhance future performance? One step will help you accomplish this in all circumstances: the DATA Check. You'll move ahead by leaps and bounds if you always perform the DATA Check after any major event or activity. It will ensure that you'll come away from even a less-than-favorable experience with a perspective that improves your next performance. Here are the elements:

DEBRIEF DETAILS

ACTION

TRAINING

ACCOLADES

We always begin by *Debriefing the Details*. This essentially means examining what was good and what was bad, what went well and what didn't. One technique for this step is simply to create a bullet-point list with two columns and begin from there. The performance could have been anything from an initial meeting with a potential client to an annual board meeting to a periodic formal evaluation in any type of organization. The debrief process is always the same.

The next step is to determine what *Action* will result from the performance. Sit down and make sure you know what just took place. Did you accomplish everything you were seeking? What is the next event that will follow as a result of what just happened? These are all questions you should be able to answer. The sooner after the event that you consider them, the better off you'll be.

Next, think about what additional *Training* you will consider. Where will you place resources for future growth? It might have a direct correlation to the substance of the meeting or encounter, or it might relate to how you'll try to handle such encounters in the future. Regardless, this is the time to commit to whatever training needs to transpire.

In his best-selling book, *What Got You Here Won't Get You There*, Marshall Goldsmith lists twenty faults that "make your workplace substantially more noxious than it needs to be." Fault number ten on his list is "Failing to give proper recognition."[1] This goes along well with our final, and absolutely necessary, step of the DATA Check, which is to give *Accolades* to those who deserve them. You must acknowledge the success of an individual or individuals. No matter what the outcome of the overall event, find something worthy of praise. Don't be cavalier about this step. It will set the tone for the future and pay dividends far longer than you may ever imagine.

PEER Performance Model Review

To review, the model begins with Preparation. Techniques pilots use include Total Immersion (Chair Flying and ATP—Available Time Potential). In the pilot's world, the phrase "over-preparation" does not exist, nor should it for you. That is followed by Smart Practice, which enables you to perform tasks as if they were second nature. The goal is to maintain Situational Awareness and to avoid Task Saturation. A technique we use to avoid Task Saturation is Equitable Time Allocation. It prevents you from focusing on any one thing for too long a period of time. The next step is Perform, whereby you demonstrate your level of mastery. The key to performing with confidence is feedback. Use a RED Check (Remove the Emotional Element; Evaluate and Find the Hidden

Value; Decide to Make the Necessary Changes) to derive benefit from even the most negative feedback. Evaluations are vital and they are the next step in the model. They must have three key elements: Structure, an All-Encompassing approach, and High Stakes. To Enhance future performance, always perform a DATA Check.

REPEAT

This brings us to the last, and most important step of the PEER Performance Model—Repeat. Performing a task only once barely allows you to scratch the surface. Performing it several times maps a path to beginning the process. Performing it repeatedly over a long period of time causes it to become second nature—an ingrained habit. Decades of watching people fly jets has made it clear that in times of maximum stress, people resort to established habits. It is for this reason that you want to form as many solid habits as possible so that you can perform flawlessly when it matters most.

FINAL QUESTION

ARE YOU WILLING TO COMMIT TO EVERY STEP OF THE PEER PERFORMANCE MODEL TO THE POINT THAT IT IS PART OF WHAT DEFINES YOU?

[1] Marshall Goldsmith, *What Got You Here Won't Get You There*, Hyperion, 2007, p.40.

8

"ROLL WINGS LEVEL"

Thunderstorms darkened the horizon, and lightning cut across the sky. Dark clouds had hung in the distance all morning, but, according to the weather report, they were threatening to move closer to the field. Neil had just hung up the phone, having confirmed with the SOF—supervisor of flying—that there were two students flying in the practice areas, both of whom were with their IPs. Two other students practicing takeoffs and landings in the pattern were flying solo. One other student was flying solo leading a formation flight of two jets, but they were just a few minutes away from entering the pattern. That was good news; he didn't want any solo students to have to navigate around the powerful storms on their way back to base.

From his vantage point in the RSU—Runway Supervisory Unit—Neil performed the duties of a tower controller for the runway used by T-38s. With his recent heavy flight schedule and this, his second time in the RSU, or "box," in a week, he felt a bit worn down, but he still didn't miss a beat when it came to controlling jets in the pattern. Seated in the controller's chair with microphone in hand, he was constantly moving his eyes to track the path of every jet in the traffic pattern. He was comfortable and in his element. Besides, he had two guests, cadets visiting from the Air Force Academy. They were on the verge of getting their hard-earned four-year degree, being commissioned as second lieutenants, and then joining a new class at a UPT base.

One of the cadets was blurting out a question, when a voice over the radio interrupted, requesting takeoff clearance. "Tiger 87, cleared for takeoff," Neil replied, giving a *don't speak until spoken to* look to both cadets. As the T-38 began its slingshot ride down the runway, the cadets moved to the edges of their seats. When full afterburners kicked in, one of the cadets gripped his stool while the other reached to brace his bottle of water, as if it would rattle right off the table.

"Captain Williamson," one of them asked, "why doesn't the main control tower monitor jets in this pattern?"

"Mainly because we need to have an experienced instructor out here watching everything that goes on in the pattern close up, particularly when students are flying solo," Neil said, tilting his head back and finishing off the last drops in his Thermos.

In an instant, another T-38 appeared on short final maneuvering for a touch-and-go, drowning out any competing sound as it blasted by the RSU.

"The bottom line is that the T-38 is not a forgiving jet—not in the slightest. It's without a doubt the most challenging, slippery jet any country has ever used in pilot training. As a result, the stakes are high, especially in the pattern where there isn't a lot of altitude to recover. It doesn't take much to get your—"

Neil stopped short and grabbed the radio. "Tiger 14 solo, go around!" he said emphatically to the solo student. He watched intently for indications that the jet was discontinuing its landing approach and going around without delay.

"Roger, Tiger 14 solo is on the go," responded the student confidently.

As the nose of the White Rocket pointed toward the sky, the gear retracted into the belly of the jet and the flaps came up. It flew past the RSU. Neil, clearly agitated, continued. "That guy was flying too low on final approach. The control tower would never have caught that in time. Another example of why there has to be a controller out here next to the runway."

The three of them watched as the jet accelerated and gained altitude.

"If that pilot comes in too low again, I'll make him do a full stop on the next trip around the pattern," Neil remarked. The puzzled looks on the cadets' faces suggested they were too busy wondering how on earth they could ever actually get to the stage of *flying* a jet like that to register his point.

Curious to find out who was flying with the Tiger 14 call sign as the entry was missing from his list, Neil phoned the SOF again. "Got it— Lieutenant Clark. Thanks." Neil recalled how Lieutenant Dewey Clark (Mace) had done a fine job on his recent formation checkride. It was always helpful for him to know the experience and skill level of students flying solo. Regardless of how well they did, though, solo students in the pattern always required the controller's full attention.

"Tiger 87, request closed," a pilot of one of the jets in the pattern said as a flash of lightning illuminated the horizon.

Neil quickly scanned the sky. "Closed approved."

"Sir, what does 'closed approved' mean?" asked one of the cadets.

"Closed is a type of pattern." He pointed to the rapidly climbing T-38 whose pilot had just made the request. The White Rocket executed a steep, climbing turn back up to pattern altitude. "The point of all that maneuvering is to get back up in the pattern so he can practice another landing," Neil added.

"Tiger 34, flight of two, initial." Hearing the female voice over the radio, Neil was cognizant of the added pressure she felt. There were so few female pilots on base that any time one flew, it was easy to assign ownership to a flawed radio call or less-than-perfect flight procedure.

"Roger, winds are one-eight-zero degrees at ten knots," Neil replied as he looked down to his call sign sheet and determined that Lieutenant Carley Macfadden (Dublin) was leading the formation.

"Captain Williamson," one of the cadets asked, "what does *initial*—"

"Standby," Neil said abruptly as the flight of two T-38s entered the pattern. He watched closely to ensure that lead did her job of flying a tight, abbreviated pattern that would allow her wingman to acquire adequate spacing and touch down a safe distance behind her. Neil mouthed the words *nice job* as Dublin flew a very aggressive and tight pattern.

As Dublin's jet touched down in front of him, he heard her engines spool up as she advanced the throttles, accelerated and took to the sky to practice another takeoff and landing. After she got airborne and raised the gear and the flaps, he heard her next radio call, "Tiger 34 Lead, solo, request closed."

"Closed approved," Neil responded, as she performed her own mini air show, aggressively raising the nose of her jet almost straight up to climb back to pattern altitude. At the same time, he monitored her wingman as he touched down and then accelerated past the RSU.

"Tiger 29 solo, initial," radioed another pilot.

"Roger, winds are calm," answered Neil. He now had time to explain that "initial" was a position a pilot reported as he entered the pattern. He pointed up so the cadets could witness Tiger 29 screaming overhead at 300 knots as it approached to perform some practice landings.

Just as Neil took his eyes off Tiger 29, he looked at the Tiger 14 aircraft.

He leaped out of his chair and knocked over his Thermos. "Tiger 14, ROLL WINGS LEVEL!" he yelled, frantically pressing the radio transmitter button. "Tiger 14, LEVEL YOUR WINGS!"

Neil had the most sickening feeling in his stomach he had ever experienced. The solo jet was rolling out of control and rapidly losing altitude. "Tiger 14, ADD FULL POWER, ROLL WINGS LEVEL, RAISE YOUR NOSE!" Neil felt completely helpless as he watched the troubled jet fall out of the sky like a brick. Having lost too much altitude, it quickly passed the point at which recovery was possible.

"Tiger 14, EJECT, EJECT, EJECT!" Neil repeated over and over. Seconds later, smoke rose from the point of impact as Neil searched frantically and saw a partially inflated parachute. The student had gotten out.

The three phone lines in the box started ringing at the same time. The red phone was a direct line to the SOF. Neil simultaneously called for emergency vehicles to proceed to the crash site with one phone while picking up the red phone. As soon as he contacted the emergency vehicle dispatcher, he dropped the handset to the floor and raised a pair of binoculars to scan the area of the crash for any movement, hoping for a chance to get a glimpse of the pilot standing up. He saw nothing but a parachute on the ground, half inflated by the wind.

"It was Tiger 14, the solo student, Lieutenant Clark. I'm looking in that direction right now but don't see anything yet," Neil responded to the SOF.

Trying to hold the radio handset and two phone lines at the same time, Neil radioed, "Attention all airplanes in the pattern, the runway is now closed. Depart the pattern and contact the tower for instructions to land on the north runway."

"Tiger Control, this is Tiger 34 Lead, solo," Dublin radioed back.

Neil worked to untangle the radio handset cord as it had become wrapped up with the two phone cords. "Go ahead, Tiger 34 Lead, solo," he replied.

"It looks like the crash site is just beyond the north service road. I see a chute but no movement by the pilot," Dublin reported, clearly shaken.

"Roger," replied Neil, who stood silently with the binoculars, anxiously searching for any sign that Lieutenant Clark had survived the crash.

CHAPTER EIGHT DEBRIEF

RISK ENVELOPE

What kind of a man would live where there is no daring? I don't believe in taking foolish chances, but nothing can be accomplished without taking any chance at all.

CHARLES LINDBERGH, AVIATOR

Mastery of Performance gives you the ability to step out on a limb, with a high degree of confidence that it will not break, even if you're teetering on the end. The point is not that the limb can't break, but rather that you've skillfully chosen the limb that is least likely to break. The previous debriefs can be summed up by two words—risk reduction. Simply put, mastery enhances your ability to deal with the unknown. Your ability to deal effectively with the unknown allows you to venture more securely outside of your comfortable area of operations. This direct result of achieving mastery dramatically increases your opportunity for success, thereby reducing risk. It frees you up to make decisions that risk-averse people just can't make. Whether you are an entrepreneur creating a start-up, a CEO running a multinational corporation, working to land the account that will change your career, or leading a group of people toward the accomplishment of a specific task, your decisions boil down to calculation of risk.

THE RISK ENVELOPE

In aviation, lives depend totally on pilots' ability to judge, manage, and reduce risk. The closer you get to duplicating this mind-set, the easier it will be for you to perform at your maximum level when needed. Consider the example of the United States Air Force jet demonstration team, the Thunderbirds, or the United States Navy's equivalent, the Blue Angels.

We have heard more than one casual observer comment on the "death-defying" or "daredevil" aspect of their spectacular air shows. In reality, their elegant display of precision, skill, and teamwork couldn't be further from death-defying or daredevil stunts. The pilots on these teams have judged, managed, and reduced risk to such an extent that a spectator's drive to the air show is far riskier than the air show itself.

Not long ago, we met with a friend, Rafael Pastor, the CEO of Vistage International, the world's largest CEO membership organization, with 15,000 members. He had recently attended an air show and watched the Thunderbirds perform. Before we began to address the planned topic of our meeting, Mr. Pastor enthusiastically relayed his impressions of what he witnessed at the air show. He commented on how his organization could benefit by mirroring the precision, skill, and teamwork the Thunderbird pilots so artfully displayed. Coming from a CEO with such impeccable credentials and vast leadership experience as Mr. Pastor, his comments give added credence to the idea of transferring such skills from aviation to the business world. If you become intentional and focused about applying the principles of this book, you'll be in good company. You'll also be among those who realize that Mastery of Performance and precise execution will allow you to operate with reduced risk, yet within a larger risk envelope.

THE REWARDS OF RISK

An example of how great the rewards of risk can be took place early in the career of legendary filmmaker George Lucas. Despite his breakout success with a movie called *American Graffiti*, which ultimately grossed over 100 million dollars worldwide, it was reported that he was at odds with the studio that was financing his next project.[1] Ultimately, *Star Wars* shattered box-office records and catapulted the brilliant George Lucas into an exalted status that few filmmakers ever have, or ever will attain. However, because he made a sequel to *American Graffiti*, which was nowhere near as successful as the previous two films just mentioned, when it came time to make *The Empire Strikes Back*, Dale Pollock writes in his book *Skywalking* that Lucas "was about to take an even greater risk ... if he failed again, he could lose everything."[2] Have you ever believed in something to the extent that you were willing to risk everything?

It is worth taking the time to consider what our society would be like without those willing to take monumental risks. Imagine how our lives would be different absent the accomplishments of people like the Wright Brothers, who ultimately "shrank" the world when they demonstrated that powered flight was possible. Or consider the example of countless entrepreneurs and business leaders who risked everything and won.

Yet no matter how successful the results of some risks are, by definition, they can never have a completely predictable outcome. Mace did everything he could to try to manage the risks involved in learning to fly jets. He was enthusiastically dedicated to every aspect of pilot training. Yet his lack of experience prevented him from understanding all the factors involved in keeping his crippled jet in the air. Regardless of how well you prepare and practice, you can only reduce risk, never eliminate it. Think about what you have done to this point in your life and career. Did you grow most when you were in comfortable, non-challenging environments? Or did a challenge launch you forward to perform at maximum ability and discover a new level of capability?

FINAL QUESTION

DO YOU RECOGNIZE RISK AS AN OPPORTUNITY OR SOMETHING TO BE AVOIDED?

[1] Howard Maxford, *George Lucas Companion*, Batsford, 1999, p.29.
[2] Dale Pollock, *Skywalking*, Da Capo Press, 1999, p.204.

MACH ONE FOLLOWERSHIP

9

GUT CHECK

The coming and going of emergency vehicles, local news crews, and speculation—spoken and unspoken—over what happened left a nervous tension in the air. Alone in his car, Neil took one last look toward the spot in the sky where he had seen Tiger 14 start its roll. He shook his head to try to clear his mind of the image, turned the key in the ignition, and headed home.

Once through the door of his apartment, Neil plopped himself in a slouch on the sofa, tossing his keys carelessly beside him instead of setting them in their usual spot on the bookcase. Letting his head fall back, he closed his eyes for a moment, then sat up and opened them again. Without something else on which to focus, the image of the tumbling T-38 grew even more vivid. He looked at his watch. *Only 6:30,* he thought. Unlike any other day of his career, he knew it would be a monumental task just to get through what remained of the night.

Uncharacteristically, he took off his watch and set it aside. He grabbed the TV remote but decided against hitting the power button. Local news coverage of the accident had been thorough, to say the least, and he had witnessed enough of the day through his own eyes.

It wasn't until he felt the hunger pangs that he realized he had skipped lunch. The afternoon had been too hectic to think of stopping for a meal. With his boots still on, he went to the kitchen and stuck a frozen pizza in the oven. Leaving black scuff marks on the floor, he grabbed a beer from the fridge and downed it in three swigs. He twisted the empty can, threw it toward the trash container—but missed—and looked out the window. The day's events flashed before him, jumbled and out of sequence.

Four hours later, lying in bed, he just wanted to be able to close his eyes and get some rest. Instead, over and over again, he saw the roll, and the fall, while reliving his radio calls to the distressed aircraft. *Tiger 14, ROLL WINGS LEVEL!* ... *Tiger 14, LEVEL YOUR WINGS!* ... *Tiger 14, ADD FULL POWER, ROLL WINGS LEVEL, RAISE YOUR NOSE!* ... *Tiger 14, EJECT, EJECT, EJECT!*

He slept restlessly while the questions ran through his mind: *Did I see the jet when it first began to roll? Did I delay even for a second? Did I give the right response? In enough time? Was I clear? Did I say what I think I said?*

Neil ripped a sheet from the bed and moved to the easy chair. Just as he settled in, he couldn't help but recount the events of the week leading up to the crash. He recalled the checkride he had given Mace. Putting a name, a face, and a voice to Tiger 14 made the accident that much more difficult to swallow. He recalled barking at Mace on his formation checkride. *"Get control of your aircraft!"*

Mace had responded well, but had Neil made the right choice in how to address him? He gave the typical tried-and-true Captain Williamson directive. *And it worked. . . . Mace flew a strong checkride.* In the bigger picture, though, how had his methods affected Mace? Neil was asking questions for which he knew there were no answers. Still, he couldn't settle his mind.

Once he did finally fall asleep, it didn't last long. Before daylight, he was awake again, with a stiff neck to top off the sleep deprivation. Maybe exercise would bring some clarity to him. He quickly dressed and headed out the door for a run.

The storm that hung in the distance the day before finally moved in. Under thick clouds, Neil started at his usual pace. Raindrops began to hit him two miles from home, and the first thunderclap reminded him of seeing lightning in the distance from the RSU the day before. It occurred to Neil he hadn't heard that thunder; the roar of the 38s had drowned it out. Before the tumbling T-38 could come fully to mind again, he changed his pace from a jog to a run. He arrived back at his front steps exhausted and soaked. Slowly catching his breath, he stood in the rain for a minute, letting it fall on his face; for a few fleeting seconds, the crash was not front and center in his mind.

A nosy neighbor poked her head out the door. "What are you doing standing in the rain like that? Are you all right?"

Neil didn't know what to say. He nodded slightly, and headed up the stairs to his apartment.

After a shower, Neil warmed some water in the microwave for a cup of instant coffee, threw away the rest of the unfinished pizza still sitting on the table, and flipped on the television. ". . . is all we know about yesterday's crash at Whiley Air Force Base . . ." He didn't hear the rest of the report. With one look at the crumpled heap of a jet and the ambulance pulling away from the site, he turned off the set. Forgetting about the coffee, he laced up his boots and left for base.

CHAPTER NINE DEBRIEF

INTRODUCTION TO MACH ONE FOLLOWERSHIP

He who has learned how to obey will know how to command.

SOLON, GREEK LAWMAKER, SIXTH CENTURY B.C.

A vital but infrequently discussed aspect of leadership is an understanding of followership. While there are various definitions of followership, we focus on what we call *Mach One Followership*—a dynamic, fluid interrelationship between a follower and leader that proactively drives toward goal attainment. The finest leaders among us were once Mach One Followers, and they routinely become Mach One Followers again whenever the situation dictates. They comfortably operate on a continuum that bridges followership and leadership; one feeds the other.

In the early 1900s, Albert Einstein's writings on relativity formed the basis of a concept of the relationship between space and time. The result was that physicists changed the way they viewed that relationship. That is to say, the two concepts came to be viewed as two parts of the same thing. The term "space-time continuum" is now commonly used. Einstein simply stated that you couldn't talk about one without including the other. The same relationship exists between followership and leadership. They are not two distinct concepts, but two closely intertwined and inseparable ideas.

ACTIVE FOLLOWERSHIP

A common thread between Mach One Followership and leadership is that both are *active*. Mach One Followers are not passive sheep, or "yes people" waiting for orders to be delivered and then dutifully carrying them out to the letter without any creative thinking or ingenuity. Mach One Followers seize the initiative, deploying their intellect and skills to complete tasks and projects with full responsibility and accountability, as if *they were the leaders.*

Mach One Followers learn and use techniques, perspectives, and information that will enable them to grow within themselves while making vital contributions to the needs of the business. At this elevated stage of followership, Mach One Followers draw upon what they have accomplished with the PEER Performance Model. That is to say, they are mastering, or have mastered something, to the point that their contributions become invaluable to the business or organization. As an additional result, the totality of what they do motivates leaders to want to become better, more effective, leaders. This is akin to what Ira Chaleff discusses in his book *The Courageous Follower: Standing Up To and For Our Leaders.* He discusses an effective type of followership in which a follower supports a leader but doesn't shy away from questioning when it becomes necessary. He describes such a follower as a "true partner with the leader."[1]

Such followers operate with great diplomacy, not getting too emotionally high or low, but focusing on the goals of the mission. When they make decisions, they often do so after receiving full input from those above and below them in the chain of command. A Mach One Follower stands above the crowd by virtue of three key characteristics that they possess: Judgment, Enthusiasm, and Tenacity. In essence, they are the *JET Set*. In a later debrief, we'll explore each of these characteristics in detail.

INCREASING MACH ONE FOLLOWERSHIP SKILLS

Like many business leaders, Neil does not occupy the highest position in the chain of command. All business leaders must answer to someone, whether it is a board of directors, shareholders, business partners, or ultimately, customers, to name a few possibilities. In Neil's case, he answers to his immediate superior, Major Herrera, the chief of Check Section, but he is beginning to realize that he needs to gain a greater awareness of his leadership style. No one remains static on the followership/leadership continuum; knowing *when* to reposition oneself along the continuum is a valuable skill to have.

Essentially, Neil experiences a leadership identity crisis that pushes him to evaluate his effectiveness. He conducts a gut-wrenching self-examination after Mace's crash. He tries to determine if, while giving the checkride to Mace, he helped the student pilot improve upon the first characteristic of a Mach One Follower—Judgment. Neil realizes that his further growth in the realm of leadership hinges upon his ability to develop better judgment in his students, since sound judgment in all situations is the point of aviation training. But how can he motivate his students if they fear his hammer-like approach to giving checkrides? He realizes that he must change something. He determines that he must develop his flexibility and self-awareness. By opening his mind and being willing to learn from the example of other leadership styles, Neil enters the fluid dynamic between followers and leaders. He is willing to step into the role of being a Mach One Follower with the goal of improving his leadership effectiveness.

FINAL QUESTION

AS A LEADER, ARE YOU WILLING TO ASSUME THE ROLE OF A MACH ONE FOLLOWER TO IMPROVE YOUR LEADERSHIP EFFECTIVENESS?

[1] Ira Chaleff, *The Courageous Follower: Standing Up To and For Our Leaders*, Berrett-Koehler Publishers, Inc., 2003, p.41.

10

THE HUMAN ELEMENT

Looking out from his adjoining office, Major Buford noticed a mixture of sadness and shock in the Tiger Flight room. The base commander had issued a stand-down order, so no flying would take place that day. As the students entered the room, Buford noticed an absence of the usual chatter. As each one passed Mace's chair, reactions varied. Some paused and touched it. Others laid private notes on it. Buford was well aware that none of them knew who was supposed to pick up the notes or what might be done with them, but it didn't matter.

The door to Buford's office was open, but he was the only one inside. The Tiger Flight IPs were already sitting at their tables in the flight room. He noticed that half of the overhead lights were malfunctioning, which seemed fitting for the circumstances.

As a former combat fighter pilot, Buford had seen many lives lost. This experience allowed him to understand how Mace's death would impact the rest of the flight. He entered from his adjoining office and proceeded directly to the podium at the front of the room, making eye contact with no one as he walked. "Let's bow our heads and have a moment of silence for Lieutenant Dewey Clark," he said simply.

Everyone did as instructed and the thoughts around the room seemed to range from reflection to respect to pride.

After sixty seconds, Buford raised his head and continued. "Yesterday at 13:31 hours, Lieutenant Clark ejected from his jet, tail number one-nine-five-two. By now you know he did not survive the ejection. He will be sorely missed. Everyone knows that his mind and heart were in the right place." He looked out at the faces before him. "Don't let what happened to him change your commitment to what you are doing here. Once you are awarded your silver pilot wings, you'll walk with confidence in each step you take and you'll hold your head up high. No matter what you do the rest of your life, first you'll always be known as a jet pilot who was willing to put your life on the line for your country." He looked at the floor in thought. "Mace's death will not be the last you'll experience as a pilot."

Buford's eyes rose to his students once more. "Every time you lose a fellow pilot, you'll be changed forever in some way. Sometimes you might be the one to console a family member. Sometimes you won't know the pilot personally, but will feel as if you did simply because there is a bond among pilots."

The students were hanging on Buford's every word. He knew what they were experiencing. They all realized that it could have just as easily been them up there in the doomed jet. Death in the line of duty was a new concept to student pilots. Most would still be in denial about the fact that their flight mate was gone, or that they, too, could lose their life while serving their country. A sense of being overwhelmed followed. Buford knew the feeling of shattered confidence all too well. When he was younger, it hit him every time like a slap in the face. Looking over the somber students, he wondered who would recover, and who wouldn't.

Regardless, he knew it was his responsibility to get them each back in the saddle ASAP.

"Today there will be no flying. I want you to sit with your flight mates and talk. Just talk. I don't want you to speculate about what may have caused Mace's crash. Talk about Mace. Talk about how fortunate you are to be here. Talk about how you will do everything with more attention to detail than you did before. Just talk.

"The services for Mace will be held in four days. Mace's wife, parents, three brothers, and two sisters will be in the front row. As his fellow flight mates, you will all be seated in the row directly behind them. I will lead a formation of T-38s that will pass overhead the ceremony and fly a missing-man formation, which consists of four jets approaching at low altitude. As the formation flies directly over the ceremony, one jet will select full afterburners and climb up and away from the other three, symbolizing Mace's departure. As they fly out of sight over the horizon, you'll see three jets with an open slot between them.

"Unfortunately, you'll witness a lot of these formations throughout your career. Each one will shake you to the core, whether you personally knew the pilot or not. But I want you to realize that you owe it to your departed aviator to take your game up a notch. That's what Mace would want you to do. That's what I want you to do now. Honor Mace's memory by being better; both with your performance in the jet and your devotion to each of your flight mates. Remember Mace. Push one another. Be better."

Major Buford left the briefing podium and walked back into his office, closing the door behind him.

Jack looked over at Dublin, who was curiously eyeing The Tenth.

"Preston, how are you doing?" she asked, focusing squarely on him.

121

Dublin punctuated the seriousness of what she said by dropping the use of his nickname.

He didn't respond right away. Dublin got up from her table and walked a few steps to take a seat next to him, adjacent to where Jack was sitting. Noting the concern in Dublin's voice, Jack angled his chair toward them.

Finally there came a response. "I should have figured this out earlier," said Preston.

"What would that be?" Dublin asked.

"That I don't belong here," he said in the most serious tone Jack had ever heard him use.

"Why would you say that? You've made it through well over half the program and you've done a great job. What makes you think you don't belong here?"

The Tenth looked Dublin square in the eye. "I'm not like the rest of you guys . . . and I'm finally willing to admit it."

Dublin's concern grew. "Mace's death has shaken all of us, but we can't let it stop us from what we came here to do. Do you think he'd want you to quit? We need to honor his memory, as Major Buford said, by kicking our game up a notch."

Again, the Tenth didn't respond right away. Dublin continued, looking intently at him. Jack listened with his head down. "Getting our wings is clearly within our grasp. Remember when Captain Williamson briefed us about beginning our sprint to the finish as we entered the T-38 phase of the program? You never give up in the final sprint to the finish line. That means giving up all that you've put into this race. You've spent a good part of your life earning your ticket to this opportunity. It only comes along once in a lifetime."

The Tenth cradled his head in the palms of both hands, his elbows resting on his legs. Such signs of despair were not common in the T-38 flight room. Jack knew something significant was going on with his friend and fellow pilot. "You can't be talking about Self-Initiated Elimination, Preston."

"Jack, I've proven to myself that I can fly jets. But I haven't proven to myself that I have what it takes to stick to it for the long haul."

Dublin leaned in closer to him. "Preston, my grandfather had a philosophy. He told me always to remember that in the scheme of things, our lifetimes are just a tiny tick mark on the endless continuum of time. In order to make that tick mark count, you need to do a few things: be able to recognize life-defining challenges when they're presented to you; come up with a plan for how to conquer those challenges; implement that plan; and, most important, never give up until you succeed."

The Tenth continued to cradle his head. "I know what you're saying makes sense, but I also know that I'm missing whatever internal drive you guys have that lets you stick to conquering a major challenge like UPT. That's always been an issue for me. When I think back, I've always allowed one thing to knock me off course."

Dublin leaned back away from him. "Preston, you sound like you're taking the path of least resistance. Just because you're experiencing some doubt doesn't mean that you have to give up."

"I see in everybody's eyes that nothing can keep them from crossing the finish line. I've been trying to convince myself that I have that same level of commitment, but now I know I don't."

"Preston, when it comes down to it, what are you really focusing on right now?" Jack asked.

"From day one, I've been trying to convince myself that I belonged here, that I could make it over any obstacle that came up. Mace's crash has me looking at everything from a deeper perspective. I see just how much is at stake when we strap ourselves into those jets. And I can't see the finish line anymore, because I can't shake my fear of something going wrong."

Dublin put her hand on his back. "Preston, we all have that internal drive that allows us to stick with something. It can be taken away only if you let it."

"What happened to Mace rang that bell of doubt inside of me, and I can't 'unring' it. I just can't." With that, The Tenth stood up and proceeded directly to Major Buford's office.

Jack knew he would never see The Tenth in a flight suit again.

CHAPTER TEN DEBRIEF

THE JET SET

Sometimes, adversity is what you need to face in order to become successful.

ZIG ZIGLAR, AUTHOR AND MOTIVATIONAL SPEAKER

It can happen suddenly, or it can develop over the course of time. When adversity strikes, one of two outcomes usually follows—either a dramatic leap forward or total capitulation, "folding the tent," so to speak. Virtually all rigorous training environments, whether a fifty-two-week jet pilot training course or a ninety-day new-hire probationary period, are designed to elicit one of these outcomes. The leader's job is to identify who will likely be able to overcome adversity and who will not.

IDENTIFYING MACH ONE FOLLOWERS

Mach One Followers know how to step up to a higher level when adversity strikes. They respond like champions, reaching deep within themselves to rise above setbacks and attain an even higher level of efficiency as they work toward Mastery of Performance. By being great followers, they learn to develop such confidence that adversity actually *elevates* them. To them, it represents an opportunity to excel.

Based on his considerable experience training pilots, Major Buford expects most students to rise to the occasion. Every action or command he gives is designed to push them forward when they are challenged to the core. However, he knows it is equally important to identify those who are not Mach One Followers as early in the process as possible.

JET: WHY JUDGMENT, ENTHUSIASM, AND TENACITY ARE VITAL

JUDGMENT

Judgment is to aviation what breath is to the body. The point of all flight training is for student pilots to develop sound judgment that will allow them to make critical decisions in the most dire situations imaginable. Likewise, in the business world, the most valuable leaders have developed sound judgment and decision-making ability. As previously discussed, followership and leadership are as inseparable as Einstein's space-time continuum. Developing judgment as a follower dramatically enhances one's ability to make decisions as a leader in the future. That's the whole point of Mach One Followership. Who is best suited to inspire a team of Mach One Followers? Clearly, a leader who has walked in their shoes.

ENTHUSIASM

Mach One Followers possess unbridled enthusiasm. They display it when others give up. When things look their darkest, they don't loosen their grip on the handle of enthusiasm. It is just such a situation that propels them forward. Mach One Followers focus on what they can achieve, not on what can stop them. Great business leaders of the past and present are often described as being driven. They have always focused on what they could achieve. They possess a great Mach One Follower characteristic: an unstoppable Internal Drive. This internal strength carries Enthusiasm from a temporary place of excitement and motivation over the "newness" of something to an enduring characteristic. One's Enthusiasm grows to provide the energy and staying power to complete difficult challenges and objectives. The Internal Drive is so deeply assimilated that it becomes an intrinsic part of the Mach One Follower.

TENACITY

After Mace's crash, Dublin and Jack exhibit the Tenacity needed to fight through their fear and trepidation.

"Mace's death has shaken all of us, but we can't let it stop us from what we came here to do," Dublin told The Tenth. *"We need to honor his memory . . . by kicking it up a notch."*

Despite the fact that The Tenth was able to make it more than halfway through pilot training with sound Judgment and strong Enthusiasm, he simply did not possess the third vital component: *Tenacity*.

He found it impossible to respond, even when Dublin laid it on the line: "You never give up in the final sprint to the finish line. Do that and you lose everything you've put into the race. You've spent a good part of your life earning your ticket to this opportunity. It comes along only once in a lifetime."

Possessing two out of three JET qualities enables many to become good followers, but not Mach One Followers. Mach One Followership requires the ability not only to rise above adversity and difficulty, but also to achieve Mastery of Performance. In business, this means switching direction when necessary, and doing so with full confidence. It also means doing whatever it takes to sprint to the finish line on a major initiative—

even if that sprint lasts for six months or more. Such effort requires sheer Tenacity, fueled by Enthusiasm and anchored by sound Judgment to make one solid decision after another.

FINAL QUESTION

ARE YOU CONSISTENTLY IDENTIFYING AND INSPIRING MACH ONE FOLLOWERS?

11

DISCOVERY

At his desk, Neil took it upon himself to review some past accident reports until it was time to meet with Captain Clemens. He was a fellow T-38 IP who took on the additional duty of serving as the squadron safety officer. He was also a member of the Accident Investigation Board. His job was to gather information about the crash and all events surrounding it, to determine ways to prevent the same thing from happening again. Since Neil was the controller at the time of the accident, he would provide a firsthand visual account to Clemens. Seeing him enter the front door to Check Section, Neil grabbed a chair from an adjoining cubicle and placed it next to his desk. As Captain Clemens rounded the corner, Neil tossed him a bottle of water.

"Neil, it's good to see you. Thanks for the water. I know we've been trying to get together for a few days, but I just need to ask you a few preliminary questions if you have time before your next flight," said Captain Clemens.

"Clem, I have plenty of time for that. Ask away," Neil replied.

"So, did you notice anything unusual as you were watching Lieutenant Clark flying in the pattern before the crash?"

Neil shook his head. "He got a little low on final once, but I told him to go around. It was a picture-perfect go-around, and on his next approach he had no problems."

"Anything in his radio calls sound unusual?"

"No, nothing."

"The board is talking about the usual flight control and flap problems. They're already having the simulator techs create a program to try to duplicate what happened. Next week I'm gonna go in one of the sims and run through all the possibilities we can come up with. We'll set it up to be at the same altitude, same fuel weight . . . basically identical conditions to Clark's jet. We'll see what happens." Captain Clemens paused. "What exactly did you see as it started to roll?"

Neil didn't hesitate. "I happened to be watching him just as he configured. The jet began to roll right around the time the flaps came down."

"Hmmm. If one flap came down and the other didn't that certainly would explain how he could roll upside down in a flash. We both know that any delay in slamming the control stick opposite the direction of the roll, even a quarter second of a delay, can put you in a world of hurt. And when you're spiraling down toward the ground, reaching the ejection handles wouldn't be the easiest thing to do either," Clemens said.

"I know. It would be a tough thing for an IP to handle, let alone a student flying solo," Neil added.

"Yeah. I remember hearing about a similar accident ten years ago when I was a UPT student; brand-new IP was flying with a student in the traffic pattern. Unfortunately, they didn't eject in time, either," Clemens said.

"Regardless of the outcome of this investigation, I think I'll start giving a low-altitude roll scenario on future simulator checkrides," said Neil.

"Not a bad idea," Captain Clemens said. "It'll be the standard six months or so until we get the final report from the accident board. Based on what I've heard so far, it sounds like a flight control problem is a strong possibility. But we all know it could also be related to a bird strike, engine failure, pilot distraction . . . who knows? Anyway, thanks for letting me know what you saw firsthand. I'll contact you if I get any news before the full report comes out."

"Let me know if there is anything else I can do for you," Neil replied.

***

As he reviewed a recent entry in the personal logbook he used to record the details of his flights, Jack froze. The numbers 1-9-5-2—the jet in which he and Captain Hinton over-sped the flaps—stared him in the face. *It's the same jet!* The realization hit like a ton of bricks through a windowpane. Just as quickly, a huge question began to flood his mind: *Could there have been a connection?*

Jack's eyes rose from his logbook as Neil passed by in the squadron hallway just outside of the Tiger fight room. Without hesitation, Jack spoke up. "Captain Williamson, you have a minute?"

Continuing to walk with purpose, Neil shouted over his shoulder, "I'm on the way to get ready for a checkride. Catch me later." Suddenly he stopped in his tracks. He paused for a moment before turning around and walking back over to Jack. "Actually I have a few minutes. Come on, follow me down to Check Section."

Together they walked in silence to Neil's desk, where he offered Jack a seat. "I appreciate your taking the time to talk to me. I know you must be busy with the investigation."

Neil shrugged. "It's no problem. I'm sorry for the loss of your flight mate. He was a good pilot."

"Yes, and an exceptional man." Jack paused to center himself. "To be honest, I'm not sure how to process all that's gone on. We all know that the stakes are high in what we're doing, but the crash has shoved that reality into our faces."

"Gaining perspective is part of the job." Neil leaned forward with his elbows up on his desk and hands clasped. "In the flying game, when something like this happens, we take a time-out to reflect, evaluate how we do things, adjust anything that needs to change, and then move on."

Jack's attention was leveled at the floor. "Sir, I can't help but question what could have caused the crash. Since you were the controller at the time, are you involved in the investigation?" He looked up to Neil. "Do you know anything yet?"

Neil leaned back into a more relaxed posture. "I gave a statement about what I saw and heard from the box, and that's about the extent of my involvement. But accident investigations are incredibly detailed. They look at every aspect you could imagine; everything from Mace's eating habits, his sleeping habits, his personal relationships, to the weather and the maintenance history of the jet since the day it entered service. They'll look into every nut and bolt of every system that was ever touched, by whom and when. There's a record of everything. If anything could have contributed to the accident, it'll be discovered."

"If you were to guess, based on what you saw from the box, what would you say was the cause?"

"Assuming it was a mechanical issue, I would guess a flap or a flight control problem, but it's impossible to know at this point."

Jack felt the need to press on. "Sir, I just learned the tail number of the jet that crashed. I'm assuming that maintenance did a thorough check after our write-up a few weeks ago."

"What write-up is that?"

"The flap overspeed that Captain Hinton and I had on a training flight."

"That's strange," Neil said. "I spoke to the safety officer and he didn't mention anything like that. But then again, I guess there would be no real reason for him to bring it up with me."

"It was a communication issue between Captain Hinton and me. He took the jet before I had time to raise the flaps, after I had just lowered them to practice a stall series. Apparently he didn't realize they were still extended. We exceeded the maximum airspeed limit for the flaps, so we terminated the flight and came back to base after doing the Structural Damage Checklist. Everything was fine and the landing was uneventful."

"Well, there's no doubt that the board will take a look at it and see if it had anything to do with the crash—"

"Does the board have the ability to determine exactly what happened?" Jack interrupted.

Neil seemed to appreciate Jack's concern. "Hard to say. As you know, unlike airliners, our jets aren't required to have Flight Data Recorders that track everything. So figuring out what happened is like putting together a puzzle—but making all the parts yourself before you can begin the process. Sometimes all an accident board can do is offer its best guess. We'll just have to wait and see."

Neil rose from his seat. Jack slowly stood up, wondering if he should press the issue further. He decided against it. "Captain Williamson, thanks for your time. I appreciate it."

"Major Buford will keep your flight informed as the board releases any information."

***

Not ten minutes later, Jack entered the Tiger flight room. Hinton was sitting alone at his table shuffling through paperwork. Jack approached and sat down. "Captain Hinton, I just had a chance to talk to Captain Williamson about the aircraft involved in Mace's crash."

"So?" Hinton responded.

"Captain Williamson is guessing that the loss of control might have had to do with a flap problem. Since it was the same jet we had our flap overspeed in, I was concerned about the possible connection."

Hinton stopped and looked up at Jack. "You told him about our flap overspeed?"

"Yes, sir, I did."

Captain Hinton leaned forward and slowly ran his hands through his closely cropped hair. He stared down at the center of the desk as if the words he *should* say might magically appear. "What was your reason for doing that?"

"I'm just looking for clarity on the loss of my flight mate, sir. My understanding is that the mechanics wouldn't have cleared the jet to fly after our flap overspeed unless everything checked out okay."

Captain Hinton's tone and body posture deflated before Jack's eyes. He stood up slowly. "Jack . . . Lieutenant Logan, I didn't enter our overspeed event in the logbook." Hinton's words were barely audible. "The jet flew well after we had our problem, and everything looked fine after we landed."

A rush of emotions swamped Jack. Anger welled up inside him to the point that he could sense the heat of his own stare on Hinton's face. He felt a greater rage than he had ever experienced. From somewhere inside of his head, he could actually hear his heart beating. He restrained himself from speaking the thoughts that rushed through his mind.

Hinton was the next to speak, and he stumbled as he did. "With accidents like this . . . sometimes it's impossible to determine the exact cause. I recommend you keep your mouth shut. . . . Wait to see what the accident board comes up with."

Hinton walked away, his head held high. For a moment Jack thought he saw him take a misstep and actually fall into the wall before catching himself and turning the corner.

Why wouldn't he write up the incident? If I report the incident now, will it look like I covered it up? Would ratting on my IP get me blackballed as a pilot? The questions were all firing too quickly; Jack sat back down to catch his breath. He knew that his behavior in the coming days would define him not only as a pilot but more so as a person. He took a deep breath and then got up and headed for the parking lot. He needed two things tonight: a strong drink, and a stronger plan of action.

The next day the drive to base differed from all others. The stoplights at which Jack waited hundreds of times now seemed surreal. Were the green and red lights "yes" and "no" answers to his big question? What would the drive to base a month from now be like? Would the action he was about to take change everything? It didn't matter; he simply had no alternative.

Jack parked in his usual spot, on the outside perimeter of the lot. He looked for Major Buford's car, almost hoping that it wouldn't be there. . . . It was. He also spotted Captain Hinton's motor scooter. Even though Hinton would be the topic of Jack's discussion with Major Buford, his presence no longer seemed relevant.

Walking into the Tiger flight room and proceeding directly to the flight commander's office, Jack noticed Captain Hinton sitting at his table and was astonished that he was shining his boots, of all things. Knowing the implications of what was about to take place, Jack felt compassion for Hinton, but he knew he had an obligation to fulfill.

Captain Chandler sat across from Buford when Jack walked into the major's office. "Sir, I *need* to talk to you." Jack's deadly serious tone completely captured Buford's attention.

Buford nodded to Chandler. "Let's finish this later." Chandler took his leave. Buford waved Jack inside.

Jack took the bold step of closing the door behind him without being directed, and then sat opposite Buford. "Sir, there's something I need to tell you. It has to do with Mace's crash."

"Go ahead, Jack, I'm listening."

Jack's voice cracked a bit. "Captain Hinton and I had a flap overspeed on a training flight a few weeks ago."

"Listen, I want you to know you don't need to be—"

Jack cut him off mid-sentence. "It was on the *same* jet that Mace crashed in."

Major Buford still didn't understand why the words didn't match the gravity of Jack's tone. "That's exactly why we have maintenance. Don't make a connection between this and Mace's crash."

"Sir, maintenance never had a chance to do their job. I found out late last night that Captain Hinton didn't write it up in the logbook."

"What?" Buford paused for a moment. "Tell me what happened."

"I was practicing a stall series and had just finished, but didn't have a chance to raise the flaps before Captain Hinton took control of the jet. He set up for a loop and started accelerating. Before I knew it, the whole airplane was shaking, and I guess that's when Hinton realized that the flaps were still down. It just happened so fast."

"How do you know that it wasn't written up?"

"I assumed that it was. But when I heard it was the same tail number, I wanted to talk more with Captain Hinton about it, just to gain some clarity on what happened. That's when he flat out said that he didn't write it up. He told me not to say anything to anyone, and I just couldn't do that."

Major Buford's head dropped until he was staring straight down at his desk. His pronounced breathing was the only sound that could be heard in the office. Jack wondered how long it would be before Buford would break the silence.

"Jack, it took a lot of courage for you to come in here and tell me all of this," Major Buford said, finally looking up again. "You did the right thing. You absolutely did the right thing."

With that, he gave a reassuring *that is all* nod. Jack stood up and moved toward the door.

"Lieutenant."

Jack turned back to the major.

"Your actions reflect honorably on your flight mate's memory."

"Thank you, sir."

CHAPTER ELEVEN DEBRIEF

MACH ONE FOLLOWERSHIP IN ACTION

I never worry about action, but only about inaction.

Winston Churchill, former United Kingdom prime minister

What happens when a Mach One Follower is tested in a crisis situation? What happens if a cover-up or lack of action ensues, and he or she not only knows about it, but has information or skills crucial to a resolution? What does it mean when a Mach One Follower steps up?

STEPPING UP

Every follower will face crucial "step up" or "opt out" situations in business and in everyday life. Many followers will look for others to lead the way, or will wait to be directed on how to act or what to say. Not Mach One Followers. When tested, they are willing to step up and to seek the truth, regardless of the personal consequences they may face. The temptation to do nothing may be present, but ultimately, it comes down to a zero-tolerance policy toward breech of standards or ethics. The Mach One Follower's personal leadership and integrity guide the way.

Mach One Followers reach their moments of realization through proactive searches for the truth. They determine what needs to be revealed or discovered and investigate in a manner that respects the chain of command. They will not usurp authority. Eventually, the moment of realization will arrive. Mach One Followers will act based on what they have learned about the situation, not based on a potentially false reality that may have been constructed by someone else.

As we noted earlier, their Internal Drive is so strong and so shaped by their character that relenting is not an option—not before they have taken the necessary steps to remedy a situation. Self-interest doesn't trump what is good for the group or organization. These are all things that set Mach One Followers apart and keep them on the path to becoming effective leaders in the future. They step up like leaders and accept accountability—whether or not they are directly responsible for the situation.

After Captain Hinton implores Jack Logan to say nothing and wait for the accident board's report, Jack's conscience comes to the forefront: *Why would he not write up the incident? If I report the incident now, will it look like I covered it up?*

Ultimately, Jack realizes that he must step up and report the flap overspeed. At the moment of decision, he places his lifelong goal of getting his wings in jeopardy: *Will ratting on my IP get me blackballed as a pilot?* The action Jack takes as a Mach One Follower perfectly demonstrates the concept of Mach One Followership. He is stepping up and engaging his leaders, particularly Major Buford, without trying to usurp control of the situation. He exercises sound judgment as he pursues answers, even if it places his flying career in peril. He is sliding forward on the followership-leadership continuum, but he remains aware of his position within the organization.

With each step he takes, Jack reflects all three components of

JET—Judgment, Enthusiasm, and Tenacity. After he learns Captain Hinton will not report the incident, he gathers information and realizes he must take action. That shows sound Judgment. Throughout the process, he maintains his Enthusiasm for preserving the integrity of his organization, even if it means he might not be able to remain in it. When he explains what he has discovered to Major Buford, Jack demonstrates Tenacity; he will not allow the truth to be swept aside, no matter what the cost. He proves himself a future leader—as do all Mach One Followers when faced with situations in which stepping up into a solid leadership role is the only acceptable alternative. All along, Mach One Followers stick to the action plan they have laid out for themselves, cutting a clear path to the objective while respecting the places and opinions of others. Mach One Followers might privately contemplate their fate, but that is not their overriding concern when they take action.

Mach One Followers are indispensable to their companies; they are the go-to people. Leaders know that Mach One Followers will take on extra responsibility and align their focus with what the organization needs time after time. Because of their unquestionable integrity and credibility, they often serve as moral or ethical compasses, both to their peers and to their leaders. Leaders have it within their power to create an organization full of Mach One Followers.

FINAL QUESTION

ARE YOU PREPARED TO SUPPORT A MACH ONE FOLLOWER THE NEXT TIME ONE STEPS UP IN YOUR ORGANIZATION?

CENTER SEAT LEADERSHIP

12

LOSS OF FOCUS

As Jack entered the flight room the following Monday morning, he looked at the scheduling board. With relief he noticed he wasn't flying with Captain Hinton. In fact, Hinton's name was no longer on the board.

Before Jack could turn around, Major Buford approached him. "You've been assigned to fly with a different IP. Captain Hinton has moved on."

Stunned at how fast Captain Hinton's departure had transpired, all Jack could do was say, "Yes, sir." He knew that "moved on" meant that Captain Hinton had lost his flying status as an IP.

Jack looked at the scheduling board to learn who his new IP was. He was pleasantly surprised that he had been assigned to Captain Chandler, who Jack thought was one of the most capable instructors in Tiger Flight.

Captain Chandler put his hand on Jack's shoulder. "I look forward to flying with you."

"Thanks, Captain Chandler, I'm looking forward to it as well," Jack replied. But inside, his own words sounded hollow, as he still felt the burden of his possible involvement in Mace's crash. He was also concerned about the possible repercussions of reporting the incident. Captain Chandler continued. "Jack, you have only a few practice flights left before your last checkride in the program. Based on your grades on your recent training sorties, I want to focus on approaches and landings when we go up today."

Jack tried to muster up some extra enthusiasm. "That would be fine."

"Okay. Let's go flying."

* * *

On their arrival back at base, the usual end-of-flight banter over the intercom between student and IP was replaced with silence. Jack was aware that Captain Chandler had expected a better performance from him, but, more significantly, so did Jack. Something was missing.

Captain Chandler tried his best to reach the core of the problem during the debrief, but without success. He addressed Jack's technical mistakes, but Jack knew they were only symptoms of a larger issue with which he was struggling.

When the day finally ended Jack headed home. He recalled his drive to base a few days earlier when he was on his way to report the logbook incident to Major Buford. The red and green traffic lights no longer suggested yes and no answers. Now all he noticed were the red, or "no," correlations. Nothing was as it was before.

Arriving in his driveway, he turned off his car and went to get his mail. This time, his key didn't work. He continued trying to turn the lock on box H until he finally realized that H wasn't his box; it was G. *Wow*, he thought. *And I'm a supersonic jet pilot? Can't wait for next week's checkride!*

***

On the last day of the following week, Jack walked back from Check Section to the T-38 squadron after completing what he had thought would be his final checkride in the program.

"HEY, LIEUTENANT!" shouted T-Bird, his words bouncing off the cement walls and linoleum floors of an empty squadron at the end of the day. "Jack, you don't look so good. What's up?"

"I don't even know where to begin," Jack replied.

"Whoa, you're the one who always knows where to begin, where to end, and everything that goes in between. You know what . . . before you fill me in, let's head over to the O'Club."

"Actually, I was gonna hang out here for a while."

"Look, I know Dublin wants to hear about your checkride and she's already over there. Come on, we'll do a group debrief."

Jack hesitated and then said, "All right, let's go."

***

When they entered, the O'Club was packed. Pilots were everywhere, talking with their hands and embellishing their flying exploits. T-Bird led Jack through a maze of cocktail tables and war-story antics before spotting Ellie, their favorite waitress. She followed them with a pitcher of beer and T-Bird's favorite concoction, the Auger In Explosion. No patron really knew what went into the drink, but it was the most popular one at the bar. With Ellie in tow, T-Bird found Dublin and the three made their way onto the patio, away from all the testosterone.

"Thanks, Ellie," Jack said as she placed their drinks on the concrete table.

Dublin noticed the deflated tone in Jack's voice. "Should I even ask about the checkride?"

"Well, my head's still spinning. Everything went fine except I went out of parameters by going too low on final approach. We didn't have enough fuel to allow me to repeat the approach, so I busted."

Everyone stared into their drinks for a moment before Dublin chimed in. "Jack, between what you went through dealing with Mace's crash and then finding out about what Hinton did, it would've been tough for anyone to be mentally prepared for a checkride."

"Yeah, but this is what we're here to do. We have to max perform in the jet regardless. We don't have the luxury of losing focus. I let these things get to me."

T-Bird had to throw his hat in the ring. "Man, you gotta cut yourself some slack. We're not superheroes. It's not our job to pretend life doesn't happen—"

"But I let it stop me from doing what I was supposed to be able to do," Jack cut in.

"You're talking from a mission perspective," said T-Bird, "but we're individuals, and we're affected by what goes on in our lives. I'm with you that the goal is to be 100 percent capable, but to do that, you have to recognize that you're also 100 percent human."

"I hear what you're saying but I just know I fell short. Period," said Jack.

"That might be right, but we're in training here," responded T-Bird. "We're learning."

Jack shook his head. "And what are you going to say six months from now when you're sitting in the cockpit of a front-line fighter? When you're flying a jet six miles up at six hundred miles an hour—*it* doesn't know whether you're in a training environment or not."

Dublin pointed them in a different direction. "Who was the check pilot you flew with?"

Jack thought for a moment. "That's another weird thing. I flew with Williamson, and it seemed like he didn't savor the bust. I know that sounds strange. But my altitude was too low on final approach, clearly out of checkride parameters. The controller made a radio call and asked us to check our altitude. At that point, I knew it was a bust, but what surprised me was that Williamson said that he wished we had fuel for another approach. He was gonna give me a chance to redo it, which is not like the Williamson we all know."

T-Bird, who could never pass up an opportunity to slam anyone who outranked him, interjected, "Jack, no one can pass a check with Williamson, even if you catch him on a good day. Now that I know you were flying with Williamson, I'm revising my position. You flew with Williamson. Of course you busted."

"Trust me, this wasn't the same Williamson. It's like a light went on somewhere and he was showing a part of himself that no one knew existed. I noticed it when I talked to him about my flap overspeed after Mace's crash. Then, even during the ground eval before my check, it was clear he wasn't trying to find a reason to bust me on the spot. It wasn't quite like flying with Santa Claus, Captain Davis, but it definitely wasn't the same ol' Captain Williamson."

"Were you the same ol' Jack?" asked Dublin.

Her question had a visible impact on him. After a considerable pause Jack answered. "No. Not even close."

Dublin leaned forward. "I know you come from a solid background. Now is the time you need to draw on that. This is your do-or-die moment."

"Everything used to be so clear to me," said Jack. "The goal and how I was going to achieve it. Now nothing is clear."

"I can empathize with what you're going through, Jack, but you can't wait too long to get back on course. You know that in UPT, *time* is not a luxury we have. We're all here to help you any way we can. Just let us know what we can do."

"I appreciate that, Dublin. The question is not will I get back on track, but will I do it in time to graduate?"

With that Jack threw a few bucks on the table and stood up. Saying nothing, he briefly placed his hands on the shoulders of T-Bird and Dublin then began the walk to his car.

CHAPTER TWELVE DEBRIEF

INTRODUCTION TO CENTER SEAT LEADERSHIP

To lead the people, walk behind them.

LAO TZU, CHINESE PHILOSOPHER, SIXTH CENTURY B.C.

Center Seat Leadership tops a chain that starts with attaining Mastery of Performance and continues with developing Mach One Followership. It signifies the high point of years of practice and preparation, and incorporates the wisdom of every experience gained and skill learned. The Center Seat Leader leads from the top, but with a perspective from the center. The term is taken from the concept of a leader who is willing to *take a center seat.*

Years ago, I (Bill) had been tasked to fly a four-star general from one base to another in a T-38. I had flown with this particular general on one prior occasion. He was the most down-to-earth and approachable general I had ever met, so I really looked forward to the opportunity to get in the cockpit with him again. Ironically, even though he had attained the highest possible rank in the Air Force, as the instructor I was the aircraft commander when we flew together. (To give those unfamiliar with military rank the proper perspective, Colin Powell and

Norman Schwarzkopf were four-star generals.) As it turned out, we had a mechanical problem in the air and had to land short of our destination at a civilian field. The general's schedule was so packed that he had to get on a commercial flight and continue on to his destination. He told me to come along with him, and that's exactly what I did.

Upon arrival at the gate, we were given our seat assignments. When I looked at our boarding passes, I noticed we had been assigned one aisle and one center seat in the same row. I quickly moved to sit in the center seat, assuming the general would want the aisle. To my surprise, the four-star general grabbed my arm and said, "Bill, I'll take the center seat." I didn't know what to say other than "Yes, sir," but by the end the flight, I understood exactly why he had done so.

Fortunately for me, the general just happened to be in a mood to discuss his leadership philosophy. He began by telling me how he so disliked the fact that after becoming a general, and as he earned more stars on his shoulder, it became more and more difficult for people around him to say what they really thought. He realized that almost without exception, subordinates—even generals with fewer stars—told him what they thought he wanted to hear. Desperately wanting to change the situation, he decided to experiment with a few things—like taking the center seat. He said he did this for two reasons; to let others know that he hadn't forgotten what it was like to be in their shoes, and to remind himself of what it was like to be in their shoes. He said he enjoyed doing things like showing up on a base, unannounced, in civilian clothes, or attending a base sporting event where people were more likely to be themselves. Detesting the fact that before all of his announced base visits, the base would be transformed with hundreds of gallons of paint, new plants, and fixtures, he tried to fit in as many no-notice visits as his schedule permitted. What he wanted to see was how things operated on a routine basis, as opposed to the artificial environment that was inevitably created just prior to his arrival.

Once we reached our destination, the parting advice the general gave me was simple. He said no matter how high up the ladder I progress, I should never forget what it's like "in the trenches," and that it's incumbent upon any significant leader to work furiously to maintain such a perspective. I thought about this for many years, and this book's discussion of leadership certainly has its roots in the wise advice I received from the general decades ago.

In our model, Center Seat Leaders have already attained Mastery of Performance in one or more areas and proven themselves to be Mach One Followers—both prerequisites of Center Seat Leadership. Such leaders see the big picture, and everyone's place in it. Center Seat Leaders inspire and instill confidence. They solicit feedback and act upon it. Their standards are clear and they maintain them by maximizing the benefits of the evaluation process. They view it as necessary to take calculated, informed risks. When they focus on risk assessment, they see their task as expanding their risk envelope, not recklessly operating outside of it. This is how they lead their organization forward.

They combine the principles and skills that Jack, Neil, Major Buford, and others demonstrate throughout this book. When they find the need to take charge, they do so with authority. They recognize the issues and challenges employees are experiencing, and they support them by working relentlessly to acquire an understanding of what best inspires and motivates each individual.

FROM ATTAINMENT TO REFINEMENT

Up until now, the Mastery of Performance–Mach One Followership–Center Seat Leadership relationship can be said to resemble a vertical line, with the objective being to attain the latter. Once Center Seat Leadership is achieved, however, it is better to imagine this continuum in the shape of a spiral, with every action and decision touching upon all three elements when necessary. Center Seat Leaders' quest for mastery enables them continually to reach higher levels in all three areas—they refine personal and professional abilities and skills every day, climbing ever higher on the spiral.

COURSE DEVIATION INDICATOR

In the cockpits of the jets that we flew, we often relied on an instrument called a Course Deviation Indicator, or CDI. Whenever we were off course, our CDI would give us a visual indication that let us know what corrections we needed to make to get back on course. We have borrowed the term CDI from aviation, since it aptly describes three crucial characteristics all Center Seat Leaders have in common and use to keep their businesses on course:

COMMUNICATE THE COURSE

DRIVE ACCOUNTABILITY

INSPIRE VERSUS INTIMIDATE

In a subsequent debrief, we will discuss each characteristic in detail. For now, just know that these characteristics will become more apparent as we dive into Center Seat Leadership.

THE MOMENT OF BECOMING A CENTER SEAT LEADER

When does one become a Center Seat Leader? In the previous chapter, Jack begins the transition from Mach One Followership to Center Seat Leadership. He is emerging from the safer cocoon of Mach One Followership into unfamiliar territory. As Jack's and Neil's experiences up to this point suggest, no one is "appointed" or "elected" Center Seat Leader. Instead, a person gets there through years of following and completing the steps we've shared in this book. Center Seat Leaders move fluidly in and out of Mastery of Performance and Mach One Followership in order to refine their leadership skills. They lead from the top with authority, accept full accountability, and at the same time maintain a center-out perspective.

FINAL QUESTION

WHAT SYSTEM DO YOU HAVE IN PLACE TO ENSURE THAT YOU MAINTAIN A CENTER-OUT PERSPECTIVE?

13

"BE THE CONDUCTOR"

While walking to his car in an introspective mood, Jack spotted Captain Williamson pulling into the O'Club parking lot. He immediately thought of the dichotomy between Williamson's brash reputation and his attitude on their checkride earlier in the day.

Neil approached Jack. "How's everything coming along?"

"Sir . . . I'm trying to hang in there."

"Let's drop the 'sir' for tonight. Do you have a second?" Neil's tone was reassuring.

"I do, sir . . . uh, I mean . . . I do."

Neil sat down on the curb and Jack followed suit. "Look, you've been carrying quite a burden on your shoulders lately. With everything that's gone on, I can understand how you might feel a bit shaken up. How are you handling all of it?"

"To be honest, not very well. I'm feeling somewhat lost."

"Care to tell me about it?"

"Well, ever since I could stand up, all I ever wanted to do was fly. As soon as I was old enough and saved the money, I got my private pilot's license and was the youngest person ever to solo from my flight school. I made more than my share of stupid mistakes as a teenager with a pilot's license, but one thing I realized early on was that I belonged in a cockpit." Jack stopped and looked up at Neil. "I felt it in every ounce of my body at the same time; there was no other choice for me. This was what I wanted to do with my life. Since then, my complete focus has been on getting my wings."

Neil nodded. "Has something changed?"

"I have to admit that I've lost some of my focus. With Mace's crash, the flap incident, and my busted checkride—well, it's the first time I've allowed other events to take my concentration off the goal of getting my wings." Jack stared at the ground as he spoke. "I feel like I'm dwelling on the negative, which I've never done before. I need to get back on course."

"Jack, you've already accomplished the first step to getting back on course—*realizing* that you're off course. Think about it in terms of flying. Unless you know that you're off course, you've got no chance of putting in a correction to get back on course. I discovered that the hard way myself recently." Neil paused for a moment. "Jack, do you mind if I share something personal with you?"

"Of course not. Go ahead."

Neil leaned back and rested his elbows on the ground. "I was a senior in college, and one night I was fulfilling the role of designated driver. It was a week before graduation when three of my closest buddies and I had just come from the last in a series of endless parties that weekend. I'd been accepted to pilot training and my friends had their paths set as well. Two were going to law school and the other was going to travel the world for a year before coming back to pursue his MBA. One member of our group, Smitty, was the most popular and the biggest partier. He was the main reason I was usually the designated driver. It was the end of a long night of celebration and we all were headed back to our apartment complex. On the way, someone wanted to stop and get some junk food, so we did. We pulled up to a convenience store. I parked and turned off the engine. Smitty was kind of out of it and said he would stay in the car. He asked me to leave the keys so he could listen to the radio. I didn't think much of it because he was in the backseat."

Jack listened with rapt attention, and Neil continued. "While we were in the store, Smitty got out of the back and jumped into the driver's seat. A witness said he sat there for a few minutes, then started the engine and drove away. The next thing we heard, from inside the store, was the thunderous sound of crushing metal. He'd pulled out of the driveway, ran a nearby stop sign, and was hit by a huge delivery truck. It took the fire department half an hour to cut him out of the tangled heap of metal my car had become."

"Oh man. What happened to Smitty?"

"He suffered severe injuries. Almost a year to the day of the accident, he died."

Jack exhaled a long and heavy sigh. "Neil, I'm sorry. That sounds like a horrible experience to have been through." Jack caught Neil's eyes and felt pressed to ask him another question. "It sounds like you feel responsible."

Neil responded quietly. "It was my car and I left the keys in it." There was a moment of silence before Neil continued. "I have relived that decision thousands of times in my mind. I spent a lot of time by Smitty's side in the hospital and then at his parent's house, where he was taken after a few weeks. His parents made it clear they didn't blame me for what happened. I didn't completely share their opinion and continued to beat myself up for quite a while.

"Finally, I realized I wasn't going to be much use in this world if I just wallowed in anguish or regret. I ultimately understood that nothing I did intentionally resulted in what had happened. Once I accepted that idea, I was able to move on with my life. I felt that I owed it to Smitty to do that. It was that repetitive kind of negative thinking that caused me to lose focus. That's why I wanted to share this story with you.

"Jack, your situation is not unlike mine. Nothing you did caused Mace's crash. You demonstrated strength of character by going directly to your flight commander when you found out what your IP had done. The checkride bust was just because you lost focus temporarily. That happens to all of us at some point."

"It's a strange feeling," said Jack. "I'm in uncharted territory now, but I know that I need to take some kind of action to get out of it. And since I've been in UPT, I've never tried to pass a checkride without having complete focus, until today."

"Jack, you can't fly a supersonic jet without focus. Remember, it's a mental game more than anything else. A machine, or autopilot, can be programmed to manipulate the controls of an airplane. It takes a skilled pilot, though, to be the conductor of the overall symphony of a flight. As a pilot, you're the conductor of the orchestra, not an individual musician. The art of flying is to coordinate all the different factors involved, from what's going on inside the jet to the outside forces acting upon it. That's what the big picture is all about. Only the conductor has the overall picture in mind, and he can do his job only if he has focus. Jack, regain your focus and . . . be the conductor."

"I certainly have my work cut out for me. I—"

"You'll be fine. Your re-check is already scheduled for next Tuesday with Major Herrera. I have no doubt you'll pass with flying colors."

CHAPTER THIRTEEN DEBRIEF

CDI

Nearly all men can stand adversity, but if you want to test a man's character, give him power.

ABRAHAM LINCOLN, SIXTEENTH PRESIDENT OF THE UNITED STATES

In his book *It's Your Ship*, Captain D. Michael Abrashoff, former commander of the USS Benfold, a guided-missile destroyer, talks about how at one point in his career he was not an aggressive listener. He describes how, over time, through feedback, he came to realize this was not an effective leadership style. He successfully made the transition: "It seemed to me only prudent for the captain to work hard at seeing the ship through the crew's eyes."[1] This center-out perspective defines Center Seat Leadership.

The Center Seat Leader considers the company's stated initiative to be a personal and professional mission. He or she finds solutions that fulfill short-term needs by delegating to Mach One Followers while focusing on the company's long-term growth. This is accomplished through the three CDI actions: *Communicate the Course, Drive Accountability*, and *Inspire versus Intimidate*.

COMMUNICATE THE COURSE

After busting his checkride, Jack openly questioned whether he would ever regain his focus to continue his quest of becoming a supersonic jet pilot. Before Neil began his transformation to Center Seat Leadership, he would have been the last person on Whiley Air Force Base to identify with Jack's predicament. Having come to the realization that his previous unyielding, top-down leadership style was no longer effective, he recognized that he needed to learn to understand what pilot training students, the "center" of the organization, needed. He made a concerted effort to connect with Jack when he saw him coming out of the O'Club. At the point in time when Jack was most in need of course guidance Neil conveyed to Jack that he had already taken the first step toward a solution—*realizing* he was off course.

Neil wanted to help him get back on course by explaining to him that "the art of flying is to coordinate all the different factors involved, from what's going on inside the jet to the forces that are acting on it." As in a symphony orchestra, he says, "only the conductor has the overall picture in mind, and he can do his job only if he has focus. Jack, regain your focus and . . . be the conductor."

DRIVE ACCOUNTABILITY

When Center Seat Leaders communicate a course, they drive and measure accountability from the center. They expect and accept full accountability from all directions: upward, where their superiors sit; downward, to their employees; and outward, to their peers and organizational interests outside the company's walls. Through this process, the Center Seat Leader provides a degree of clarity that makes it simple for everyone to know what to expect. The result is empowerment among all members of the organization. Since everyone remains accountable, there is a sense of unity toward attaining goals, as opposed to focusing on assigning blame when something goes wrong. At the same time, this environment of mutual accountability encourages innovation, as both credit and blame are shared.

In his book *Good to Great*, Jim Collins describes how the highest level of leaders in his model, Level 5 leaders, view accountability. "Level 5 leaders look out the window to attribute success to factors other than themselves," he writes. "When things go poorly, however, they look in the mirror and blame themselves, taking full responsibility."[2]

In any situation, the "troops" will always standby a Center Seat Leader who openly accepts accountability. For an illustration of this, simply consider the stark contrast between the beloved founder of Southwest Airlines, Herb Kelleher, and Dennis Kozlowski, the former head of Tyco. It is widely known that Herb Kelleher was the embodiment of responsibility and accountability. He would not hesitate to clean planes or help gate agents when he traveled. His employees knew what he expected from *them*, but, more important, they knew what they could expect from *him*. Dennis Kozlowski, on the other hand, ended up in court. He became infamous for displays of extravagance.[3] Which of these leaders do you think stood a better chance of gaining resounding employee support when the company faced a challenge?

INSPIRE VERSUS INTIMIDATE

The third characteristic of Center Seat Leadership is the ability to inspire. Why are Center Seat Leaders so well equipped to inspire? There are two reasons. They have achieved Mastery of Performance and have spent a period of time as Mach One Followers on their journey toward leadership. This prerequisite of achieving Mastery of Performance will earn Center Seat Leaders the respect of subordinates, but it is not enough on its own to make them inspirational leaders. Leaders need the additional ability to identify with key followers. The experience of fulfilling the role of a Mach One Follower gives Center Seat Leaders a keen ability to identify with subordinates, recognize how and what they need to be inspired, and then provide the inspiration. Subordinates want to be understood by their leaders. If leaders don't understand their followers, they can't even begin to know how to inspire them. In his book *Principle-Centered Leadership*, Stephen Covey writes, "Perhaps the most powerful principle of all human interaction: genuinely seeking to understand another deeply before being understood in return."[4]

As we examine Neil's leadership journey it becomes apparent that he possessed the ability to identify with student pilots, but it was dormant and waiting to be awakened.

It was a concept that Neil was on the verge of beginning to understand.

FINAL QUESTION

IF EVERYONE IN YOUR ORGANIZATION WERE ASKED, WHAT PERCENTAGE WOULD SAY THAT YOU CLEARLY COMMUNICATE THE COURSE?

[1] Captain D. Michael Abrashoff, *It's Your Ship*, Business Plus, 2002, p.44.

[2] Jim Collins, *Good to Great*, HarperCollins Publishers, Inc., 2001, p.35.

[3] Robert P. Gandossy and Jeffrey A. Sonnefeld, Editors, *Leadership and Governance from the Inside Out*, John Wiley and Sons, 2004, p.6

[4] Stephen R. Covey, *Principle-Centered Leadership*, Simon & Schuster, 1992, p.272.

14

THE REAL THING

"**T**iger 96, you are cleared to the TORRY holding fix, hold southwest, ten-mile legs, report entering holding," stated the controller.

"Roger, Tiger 96 cleared to hold at TORRY," Jack responded.

From his position in the front cockpit, Major Herrera said, "Okay, Jack, I have the aircraft. . . . Get your approach charts out and take a look at what you're preparing to fly."

"Roger, sir, you have the aircraft."

Approaching the holding fix, Jack reviewed his chart and experienced a moment of sheer panic. For a fraction of a second, what he saw on the chart didn't match the holding pattern he was preparing to fly. His sense of shock traveled from his head to his toes. Almost instantly, however, Jack realized he was looking at the wrong depiction. Catching the mistake, he recovered quickly from the paralyzing panic and regained his composure. Only for a fleeting moment did he consider the potentially dire consequences of busting his re-check. He fought hard to keep his mind clear of such thoughts.

"Tiger 96 is entering holding at TORRY, at five thousand feet," Herrera radioed to air traffic control.

"Roger, Tiger 96," replied the controller.

Over the intercom, Major Herrera said, "Okay, Jack, I'm going to give the aircraft back to you and I'd like you to set up for another—"

Jack suddenly heard a series of thumps, felt a vibration he had never before experienced, and heard a strange whining sound coming from one or both of the engines. In his peripheral vision, he saw a flurry of feathers. There appeared to be blood on Major Herrera's helmet. He wondered if it was from the birds that had apparently come through the windscreen, or if it was Herrera's own. Looking forward from his position in the rear cockpit, Jack saw Herrera's head slump forward. Simultaneously, he felt the jet descend and noticed it turning to the left.

"Major Herrera, are you okay?" Jack yelled over the intercom system.

There was no response.

Jack's eyes rapidly transitioned between checking his instruments and straining to see Major Herrera in the front cockpit. All he could see was the very top of the major's helmet, covered with blood.

"Major Herrera, can you hear me, sir?" Jack shouted over and over. He grabbed the control stick and returned the jet to straight and level flight.

Just as he did, the Fire Light for the right engine illuminated.

Maintain Aircraft Control, Analyze the Situation, and *Take Appropriate Action* played through Jack's mind. He performed the first two steps simultaneously. He brought the throttle associated with the right engine—the one with the fire indication—back to the IDLE position as called for in the Boldface procedure. The light extinguished. Jack knew he could keep the engine running at IDLE so long as the Fire Light stayed out.

He continued to assess the situation as he turned to the pages in his checklist that addressed Engine Fire and Single-Engine Landing. If he had learned anything during the previous year, it was that following the right checklist, at the right time, could save his life.

His next step was to make a radio call to Approach Control, which handled all the air traffic arriving at Whiley Air Force Base. Jack knew they would be able to put him in touch with his squadron via radio to get additional help.

"Approach Control, this is Tiger 96 declaring an emergency."

"Tiger 96, this is Approach Control, go ahead."

"We've had a massive bird strike. I'm a student and it looks like my instructor, in the front cockpit, was knocked unconscious. I think at least one of the birds also went into my right engine. I had an indication of a fire, but that went away and I'm operating that engine at IDLE power. My remaining engine looks fine for now. I'm requesting vectors to final approach."

Jack's memory immediately flashed back to the first simulator mission he flew in the T-38 where he encountered an engine fire—the one where he had shut down the good engine and had to eject. The last thing he could do now was eject with Major Herrera unconscious in the front seat. His heart raced an additional twenty beats per minute, but he continued with laser focus on the task at hand.

"Roger, Tiger 96, I copy your emergency. Turn left to a heading of three-zero-five degrees. You are twenty-five miles from Runway Two-Seven. Standby and I'll get an instructor pilot from your squadron on the line," replied the controller with an anxious voice. For a moment, the controller's shakiness worried Jack, but he moved beyond it. He could spare no brain cells to devote to such a matter. "Tiger 96 turning left to three-zero-five degrees," Jack replied.

Another voice came over the radio. "Jack, this is the supervisor of flying, how do you read me?"

"Captain Williamson, is that you?"

"Yes, Jack, it is. I've been monitoring your conversation with Approach Control. Have you gotten any response from Major Herrera yet?"

"No, sir." Jack's voice was calm. "His head is slumped forward and I can see blood on his helmet. I think a bird came right through the front windscreen. We also took one in the right engine. My left engine seems fine for now."

"Jack, I copy your situation. I see that Approach Control is vectoring you to final. You're down to one engine and you need to get on the ground ASAP. How are you doing on your emergency checklists?"

"I've completed the Engine Failure, Bird Strike, and Single-Engine Landing Checklist and I've reviewed the Single-Engine Go-Around Checklist."

"Good job, Jack. Now we really need to talk about something you've never done before—landing from the rear cockpit."

"I'm with you on that one, sir. I can't see very much looking straight ahead," Jack responded.

"That's right," replied Neil. "You'll have to rely on looking out both sides of the cockpit *and* on your instruments. I want you to fly an instrument final; follow the vertical and lateral guidance all the way to touchdown. From looking out the sides, you'll know when you're just about ready to touchdown. Don't let it get to you, it'll look different from what you're used to. Just do your normal landing and flare procedure when you get close to touching down."

"Okay, I copy. I'll keep a close eye on my instruments throughout the approach and hopefully pick up some visual cues when it's time to flare and touchdown. I've reviewed the Single-Engine Landing procedures and I'm ready."

"Tiger 96, this is Approach Control. Turn farther left to a heading of two-eight-zero degrees. You are cleared for approach to Runway Two-Seven. When you roll out you'll be on a ten-mile final. Contact the tower now, sir, and good luck."

"I'll contact the tower at this time," Jack replied. "Whiley Tower, this is Tiger 96 emergency, checking in with you."

Whiley Tower responded, "Tiger 96, you are now nine miles from touchdown. Winds are calm. Cleared to land on Runway Two-Seven. Emergency vehicles are standing by."

"Understand, cleared to land. I'll be stopping straight ahead on the runway."

"Tiger 96, sounds like a good plan. That's approved."

"Jack, this is Captain Williamson, I'm with you now on tower frequency. I'm in a vehicle at the end of the runway, and I'll give you any guidance you need. Hang in there, you can do this."

"Yes, sir," responded Jack. "All the checklists are complete. I'm ready."

Jack continued to try to get a response from Major Herrera, but to no avail. Now he needed to concentrate on performing the most challenging landing he likely would ever face. "Tiger 96, this is Whiley Tower, you are now five miles from touchdown, winds are still calm, and you're cleared to land. Good luck, sir," relayed the tower.

"Gear down and cleared to land, Tiger 96," Jack responded.

He knew a lot was riding on his ability to get this crippled jet on the ground safely, not the least of which was the fate of Major Herrera. He could feel his blood pumping throughout his body, yet he felt controlled and confident that he was up to the task.

"Major Herrera, can you hear me?" Jack shouted over the intercom, still hoping for any kind of response.

Nothing.

"Jack, you're a bit high. Keep her coming down, but don't develop a high sink rate," Neil said.

Jack was too focused to respond with anything more than a "Roger" over the radio, but he heeded the advice and lowered the nose of the jet ever so slightly, making certain he didn't descend too rapidly toward the runway. His mind chattered away. *Jack, you've practiced countless Single-Engine Landings while Chair Flying, in the simulator and in the jet . . . but you never imagined doing one for real, with your IP unconscious . . . and from the rear cockpit. . . . How do the IPs do it on a regular basis from back here? . . . I can't see a thing!?*

"Jack, you're still a little high. . . . Bring her down a bit."

Jack heard and processed the call from Neil, yet now he was unable to respond at all, as he needed to focus entirely on flying the jet onto the runway and stopping it before he sped off the end. He reduced the power slightly to continue the jet's descent.

I can't see a thing. . . . All of Jack's available senses and instruments indicated he was on course to touchdown on the asphalt, not the dirt that was on either side of the runway. He strained to see out the front of the jet, but his helmet met the canopy before his eyes were able to get a good look. He relied on his altimeter to indicate how many feet remained until touchdown. Everything was happening so fast. He intermittently glanced at the altitude pointer as it passed through 300 feet to touchdown, 200 feet to touchdown . . .

"JACK, WATCH THE . . ." Neil shouted.

At the same moment, the main wheels of Jack's jet slammed onto the runway. It wasn't pretty, but it didn't have to be. It was an emergency Single-Engine Landing by a student who had never landed from the rear cockpit. Jack used all the remaining strength in his body to apply the brakes as the crippled jet sped down the runway. Out of the corner of his eyes, he saw a blur of flashing red lights as fire trucks careened down each side of the runway trying to guess where he would eventually come to a stop.

Finally, his wheels made their last revolution. With blinding speed, emergency personnel opened the front cockpit canopy and tended to Major Herrera. Jack simply sat there, motionless, not even remembering to raise his own canopy.

Jack saw Major Herrera's arms move as he was lifted out of the cockpit. For the first time since the bird strike, he felt some relief. Finally remembering to open his canopy, he watched as emergency personnel anxiously tried to get to him. With all the commotion, Jack wasn't able to hear what Neil was saying as he stood a few feet away, but he didn't need to. Neil looked directly at him and snapped a congratulatory salute that was the most welcome sight Jack had ever seen. He was just about to raise his helmet visor, but he decided it would be better to leave it down; his emotions, which had been flying a few miles behind him, caught up with him at last. He felt a boulder-size lump in his throat, but this time it was pride rather than fear that took away his ability to speak.

CHAPTER FOURTEEN DEBRIEF

SLIDING FORWARD ON THE CONTINUUM

You gain strength, courage and confidence by every experience in which you really stop to look fear in the face. You must do the thing you think you cannot do.

ELEANOR ROOSEVELT, FORMER FIRST LADY

Center Seat Leadership is not something we are born with. It comes about as leaders evolve through experience. "Leaders learn through tests and challenging situations—not from things with which they're already familiar,"Robert J. Thomas writes in *Crucibles of Leadership.*[1]

Leadership lessons are learned by evaluating every experience or incident with feedback and implementing the findings, not just experiencing situations and forgetting about them. An old analogy about experience demonstrates this principle quite clearly. It compares two pilots, each with a certain amount of experience; for this example, let's say ten years. The first pilot has accumulated a decade of flying time, but he stopped actively learning at the end of the first year. The other pilot continued to learn each year, building upon the experience of each previous year. He is a ten-year pilot with ten years of lessons under his belt, compared to his counterpart, a one-year pilot who has repeated the same lessons, skills, and responses to situations ten times over. The pilot who has built upon his experience year after year exemplifies the Mach One Follower who has transitioned into a Center Seat Leadership role.

An intriguing aspect of leadership lessons is that, in many instances, they are not recognized or understood at the time they occur. We don't have the advantage of 20/20 hindsight when we are immersed in the present moment. The seeds are planted, to be reaped only when the time is most opportune—perhaps even decades later. Seeds can even be planted from doing the wrong thing, at the wrong time. In the words of Henry Ford, "Failure is the opportunity to begin again, more intelligently."[2]

All experience is useful in shaping leaders. Jack exemplifies this dynamic. He steps up to the plate in a true life-or-death event. His skillful handling of the situation in which Major Herrera loses consciousness in the cockpit propels him into the role of a Center Seat Leader. By the time he opens his canopy at the end of the flight, the "Jack" that occupies the cockpit seat is not the same Jack who began the flight less than an hour before.

In this single emergency flight, all three CDI characteristics come into play. Jack is left with no option but to decide upon and then *Communicate the Course*. His previous Mastery of Performance, i.e., his ability to fly the jet as if it were second nature, allows him to become the "conductor," to think strategically about the overall plan. He communicates the plan to the controller and to Neil, who was serving as the supervisor of flying that day. Driving Accountability comes into play as he shoulders the responsibility for himself, the unconscious Major Herrera, and the other people on the ground who might have been killed had he not been able to get the jet safely back to the runway. As a result of his heroic handling of the bird strike, Jack becomes an Inspiration to everyone on base. He proved to the instructors that what they were teaching undoubtedly works. He showed his fellow students that all the preparation and practice they had been doing was worthwhile. He inspired others by being an example of how they all should perform if they were ever confronted with such a situation.

EMERGENCE

By exhibiting all three CDI characteristics, Jack slides forward on the continuum from Mach One Followership toward Center Seat Leadership. Mach One Followers become Center Seat Leaders when their personal leadership merges with the organization's objectives, and they provide wise and decisive direction in a manner that inspires those around them.

FINAL QUESTION

ARE YOU PREPARED TO HANDLE YOUR VERSION OF AN "EMERGENCY FLIGHT" THAT INEVITABLY LIES IN YOUR FUTURE?

[1] Robert J. Thomas, *Crucibles of Leadership*, Harvard Business Press, 2008, p.40.
[2] John Blaydes, *The Educator's Book of Quotes*, Corwin Press, 2003, p.151.

15

THE UNIVERSITY WITH WINGS

R*oom 324, room 322, room 320*, Neil counted to himself as he followed a green line down the hallway. *There it is . . . room 318.* He felt as uncomfortable as any other pilot in a hospital setting, associating the environment with one that threatened his flying status.

Neil entered the room. Major Herrera seemed to be resting, so he quietly closed the door behind him, removed his jacket, and took a seat in the lime-green vinyl chair at the foot of the bed. In addition to the décor of decades past and the unmistakable aroma that filled every hospital, Neil noticed a classic hospital meal on a tray, with its plastic wrapping intact.

Looking in the direction of the untouched food, Herrera opened his eyes and said, "What kind of bribe would it take to get you to eat that for me so they'll think I'm getting better and let me outta here?"

"At your pay grade, I don't think you could afford what it would take to get me to eat that!" Neil was delighted to see that Herrera was back to his old witty self. "You look great. I was expecting you to be all bandaged up."

"Hey, I would have been out of here twelve hours ago," grumbled

Herrera, "but they're making me stick around for twenty-four—I don't know, they claim it's for *observation* or something. Give me a break."

The two men looked at each other for a few moments before either spoke. Neil smiled. "So, what happened up there?"

Herrera struck a pose, one arm partially extended and the other straight out in front of him as he spoke in a stage voice. "Up in the boundless sky, there I was—" His dramatic presentation was interrupted when Neil choked on a sip of water. They both broke out in laughter and the single bandage on Herrera's forehead popped loose.

Settling down, Herrera continued. "Okay, okay, in all seriousness, I was sitting in the front cockpit giving Lieutenant Logan a navigation checkride—obviously not the most exciting thing we do in the White Rocket. At one point, I saw a spec on the horizon, and that spec turned out to be a flock of birds. In the next instant, I was out."

"That's it?"

"What do you mean?"

"I mean no high-G maneuvering to avoid the flock of birds? No heads-up command—pardon the pun—to your student just before impact? Nothing but simply sitting there and taking the hit with your head?" teased Neil.

"I'm afraid so. No drama. I was just a target."

"Boss, we're gonna have to embellish that story. . . . I mean, think about it. You made the local news, now there'll be pictures all over the base of the hole in the windscreen—blood and all—and the only part you played was to use your head as a target for the unlucky bird that made it into the cockpit. It's just gonna take more to convince people to buy you drinks in the bar than a story like that."

Herrera laughed. "I'll be lucky to get a warm leftover beer. All the drinks will be going to Logan."

Herrera adjusted his position—more upright—looking not unlike the way he did sitting behind his chief of Check Section desk. Neil sensed the conversation was changing direction, but he didn't know what to expect. "So, talk to me, Neil," he said. "I've seen some big differences in you lately—some positive differences. What's been going on?"

"Come on, boss, the focus here is on you, not me."

"Captain!" Herrera said jokingly, but with a serious undertone. "We both know I'm fine, and I'll be out of here as soon as the medical wizards around here figure that out. Answer my question."

Neil tapped his fingers on his leg and took a few moments to think about that unexpected question before he replied. "I've had my eyes, or I should say my mind, opened to a lot of things lately, that's for sure."

"Go on."

"Without a doubt the turning point for me was Mace's crash. Even though I had given him only one checkride and wasn't the instructor who flew with him every day, his crash changed my view of everything I do. Then an idea finally dawned on me: Everything we do as instructors and check pilots can radically affect the lives of our students. I mean, I always knew that was true, but I never really had it in the forefront of my thoughts, and certainly not every day."

"That's something they don't emphasize too much in instructor school, do they?"

"Well, if they did, I missed it. I was concentrating more on improving my flying skills than I was worrying about the long-term influence I would have on students," Neil said.

"It's funny how we see what we look for, isn't it? You went to school to learn how to fly as an instructor pilot. But the real mission was to teach you *how to teach*; and that's the part you minimized because you were more focused on your own performance."

Neil responded, "I understand that at this point we still don't know what caused Mace to crash, but what if one thing that one instructor did or didn't do could've made a difference? My point is that the better we are at teaching, the more receptive our students will be to learning. I'm not sure why I didn't get that before. We're accountable for what happens in the jet, and for keeping them alive. I finally figured out that our job is to know what it takes to get the best out of them, instead of searching for a reason to wash them out. Am I making any sense?"

"Absolutely. You're talking about leadership—real leadership," Herrera said. "Your job is not only to set the standards and hold students accountable, but more important to figure out what it takes for them to deliver their best performance. This is especially true when the pressure is on during a checkride—more of a 'center-out' than a 'top-down' approach."

"I wasn't quite able to put it like that, but I guess that's what I'm saying."

Neil peered out the window and spotted a T-38 as it entered the overhead traffic pattern. For the first time he thought more about the perspective of the student in the jet than the magnificence of the machine.

"Neil, these concepts don't come easily to full-throttle jet jocks like you, and they certainly don't come overnight. Leadership lessons are just that: lessons. You have to be on the lookout for them."

Neil rested his chin on his closed fist.

Herrera continued. "I'm going to ask that you do one thing for me, but really it's *for you*."

"Of course—"

"I know how you totally immerse yourself in all things flying, and that's taken you to the top of the stick-and-rudder world. But now you see that this door to learning about leadership is wide-open, right in front of you. Let's face it, flying high-performance jets is a younger man's game, and we won't be in the cockpit forever. But what we learn about how to follow and how to lead will stick with us the rest of our lives. Pour yourself into it. Keep your eyes open. Use the leadership styles that work, and more important, never forget the ones that don't. You can't go a day without seeing examples all around you. Make that journey a part of you."

Neil nodded his head in agreement.

Major Herrera added, "Neil, you are ready for this. You've mastered flying, you've mastered following, now begin the journey of mastering leading—and trust me when I say that journey is one that is never-ending." Herrera paused. "There's one more thing. I'll let you in on a little secret. Don't think that flying principles apply only to the cockpit. They apply to life. Why do you think they call the T-38 the 'university with wings'?"

As Neil began to answer, Herrera interrupted. "Enough. Done. I'll see you tomorrow."

With mock formality, Neil replied, "Yes, sir," smiled, and left the room. He retraced his steps through the maze of the hospital corridors; his pace was slower than when he entered. He had a lot to think about.

CHAPTER FIFTEEN DEBRIEF

PIVOTAL LEADERSHIP EVENT

The task of the leader is to get his people from where they are to where they have not been.

HENRY KISSINGER, FORMER U.S. SECRETARY OF STATE

Not everyone attains Center Seat Leadership along the straight-arrow path that passes through Mastery of Performance and Mach One Followership. Some leaders grow into Center Seat Leadership from another leadership style. Their transition is more lateral than vertical, and usually follows a pivotal event that causes them to question their leadership style or exposes them to a style they had never before considered. We call this a Pivotal Leadership Event, or PLE.

PIVOTAL LEADERSHIP EVENT

A PLE is a significant event that affects one's leadership style. It is something that usually results in a dramatic improvement of a leader's effectiveness. In the case of Center Seat Leadership, a PLE moves leaders upward in their knowledge or insight and increases their ability to lead with the right perspective. For a Center Seat Leader, that means a perspective from the center. The changes that both Neil and Jack have undergone clearly illustrate this shift. They change forever as a result of the PLEs they experience.

Many business and organizational leaders are like Neil—set in their tried-and-true leadership ways, until a major event or incident shakes their business and/or personal life to the core.

When that happens, Mastery of Performance alone does not solve the problem. Leaders realize that they must become Mach One Followers in their own "leadership school," as Neil does. His old style of leadership will no longer serve him; he stands at a turning point. He not only experienced a PLE, but he also took swift action as a result of it.

Everyone experiences PLEs, but not everyone acts upon them. What makes the difference? The action step. But what exactly is an action step? There are two parts: the *commitment* to take action; and actually *taking* the action. In order for the action to be effective, it must be initiated a relatively short period of time after the commitment is made. Human nature dictates the more time that elapses, the less likely it is that the action will be completed. So don't delay when faced with this kind of situation.

The type of activity or action we are talking about here can fundamentally change the path of your leadership style. Using another example from the story, consider Neil's reluctance to see the human side of student pilots. Having little interest to see things from their perspective, he had no chance of being able to inspire them. As a check pilot, it was his job to evaluate their ability to meet the standards of pilot training. Prior to the crash, he rarely considered the human element as part of the equation. After the crash, something within him was awakened. He realized there was more to student pilots than how they performed on checkrides. He remembered that, just a few years earlier, he had been in their shoes. Unfortunately, perhaps as a result of trying to become the best pilot *he* could be, he had lost the ability to identify with them and to see anything from their perspective.

Upon his realization, Neil took a vital action step that affirmed his transition to Center Seat Leader: he reached out to Jack after his busted checkride. A PLE can change a leader's style in a very short period of time. In Neil's case, it happened in a matter of days.

A PLE experience also puts an effective leader on the lookout for the next PLE. As a result, he is equipped and ready to move to an even more effective level of leadership at the next opportunity. Recall that Major Herrera tells Neil, "Leadership lessons are just that: lessons. You have to be on the lookout for them."

NEVER LEFT BEHIND

Center Seat Leaders constantly bolster their personal and professional skills. They actively seek to identify situations in which their leadership is required and from which they can learn something new. They go through PLE experiences by learning and acting upon them. They are willing to take whatever action is required—a key characteristic that reflects the Internal Drive we previously discussed. They become Mach One Followers when acquiring new insight or information, and engage in PEER Performance Model activities to make new leadership skills second nature. Effective leaders will not mire themselves in a leadership style that doesn't work. Center Seat Leaders are effective because they are willing to adapt, change, and do whatever it takes to become better leaders that have a lasting, significant impact.

FINAL QUESTION

ARE YOU PREPARED TO TAKE SWIFT ACTION THE NEXT TIME YOU'RE FACED WITH A PLE?

16

"I SALUTE YOU"

Jack entered the flight room and was surprised at the surreal feeling he experienced. In less than twenty-four hours, he would be wearing the wings of an Air Force pilot, something he had dreamed about for as long as he could remember. Unlike the previous occasions when he was the first to arrive, all of the lights were on; the chairs were perfectly positioned at the briefing tables. The magnetic nameplates of the current Tiger Flight students had all been removed. The scheduling board had been wiped clean, ready to track the progress of the next set of student pilots who were about to wear the Tiger Flight patch.

Having literally stopped in the middle of the room, the events of the last six months he had spent flying the T-38 raced through his mind. The room seemed to spin around him like a carousel as he reminisced. One row of overhead lights began to flicker then went dark, just as they had the day Major Buford addressed Tiger Flight after Mace's crash. A full spectrum of emotions flooded Jack's mind. He thought about everything from the tragedy of Mace's crash to the cocky irreverence that would serve T-Bird well as he went on to join the fighter pilot community as an F-15 pilot.

He then began to consider what the *next* six months would be like. He looked over at one of the briefing tables and tried to imagine sitting on the other side, the IP side. He wasn't quite able to form that mental image; however, he was comforted by the thought that his good friend, Dublin, would also be returning with him as a T-38 IP.

* * *

Major Buford and the IPs entered from the flight commander's office one last time. The students sprang to attention, no less sharp than they were on day one. Buford began with his predictable "Take your seats" opening line, only today he sounded more like a proud father than a military commander.

"Tiger Flight, you made it." The flight room erupted with hoots, yells, and claps. "All right, all right, settle down, you still have to get through one more day with me," he continued with a chuckle. "Your flight entered UPT almost exactly one year ago with thirty students. By the time you got to the T-38 squadron you were down to twenty-five. Twenty-three of you made it to the end. Some will call you the lucky ones, but you know better; luck had very little to do with it.

"You showed up on base with hopes of fulfilling a dream that most of you have had for as long as you can remember—to earn the wings of a jet pilot. In the first few weeks of UPT, the Air Force revealed the gauntlet you'd have to progress through toward achieving that seemingly impossible goal. You realized in fairly short order that the Air Force had told you *what* you needed to master, where you needed to follow, and when you needed to lead, but the *how* was largely left up to you. Each of you was successful in doing what it took to get the job done, and you went about it in twenty-three different ways. You prepared. You practiced. You performed. And then you passed your evaluations.

"From here, some of you are going on to fly single-seat fighters. Some will fly large transports with a full crew. Some will come back here as IPs. Regardless of where you go, you'll always need to do what you were taught in kindergarten—work well with others. Never forget that. And always remember that leaders are not born into their position. They are brought to the forefront through hard work and determination; through respecting themselves as much as those around them. Your role here in UPT was to be dynamic followers as you planted the seeds of your leadership development. Now you have all exemplified leadership. To remain leaders, though, you'll need to master new skills and learn to be good followers again. Do that repeatedly and you will lead others in new directions. No matter how high up you go, you'll always be accountable to someone, so never let your head get too big!"

The room filled with a low scattering of laughter. After everyone quieted down, Major Buford continued. "There's also a saying that if the military wanted you to have a spouse, they would have issued you one. Don't take that to heart. It took me a few tries to get it right. . . ." This time Buford joined in the laughing but put his arms up to regain his momentum. "But seriously, never leave your family out of the equation. Service to your country will come before all else—it just has to be that way—but take every opportunity to include your family in all your major decisions. Do this before it becomes too late. Remember, at the core of everything you do as an officer and pilot will be how you interact with people. You can't achieve greatness alone; you can't even achieve mediocrity alone."

He looked up at the familiar faces before him. "I'm proud to have known each and every one of you. You have earned the honor that will be bestowed upon you tomorrow when those silver wings are pinned on your chests. With those wings our country will trust you with multimillion-dollar machines, as well as the lives of those with whom you serve. Devote yourself to mastery. Value followership. Lead with integrity. Tiger Flight, I salute you."

AFTERWORD

What a journey it's been! It will be helpful to take some time to consider the dramatically different paths of the characters in the story. From the full spectrum of Jack's progression to Neil Williamson's transformation, to the plight of The Tenth that resulted when he realized he was missing the single characteristic of *tenacity*, each has something worth contemplating. No doubt, there are times when we've all lacked a characteristic of Mach One Followership or Center Seat Leadership. But you've just finished reading a story that will help you reflect upon and articulate your own journey.

Never forget the relationship between these three main concepts of Mastery of Performance, Mach One Followership and Center Seat Leadership. The best leaders among us become Mach One Followers when the situation dictates. Use the PEER Performance Model not just for the obvious, but for the less obvious as well. Use it not only for learning how to do something better, but also for how to become *someone* better. Use the model to evolve into being a better follower *and* a better leader. The type of followership and leadership we discuss are not separate concepts; rather, they reside along the same continuum. Never underestimate the power you will gain by understanding the relationship between them.

One of the best illustrations of the concepts in our book occurred on January 15th, 2009. The world was treated to a magnificent display of Mastery of Performance, Mach One Followership, and Center Seat Leadership. People were glued to their news sources as the details of US Airways Flight 1549 began to filter out. First, we heard that an airliner had experienced a major bird strike. Next, the word was that it had lost both engines shortly after takeoff over one of the most densely populated areas in the world. It wasn't until even later that we began to hear the specific details. And, the details verified what many of us had suspected—that the crew had performed flawlessly under the most extreme pressure they'd ever experienced in their lives. Major news outlets informed us that the pilots had maneuvered their silent, gliding airliner to the only place they could touch down without hitting any structures or people—the Hudson River. Then we learned that the swift and skillful actions of the crew resulted in saving all 155 lives on board the aircraft. All this on a flight that lasted less than six minutes! How could this have happened?

We've all heard the term "an accident waiting to happen." This was a "success waiting to happen," the seeds of which were planted decades earlier. Captain Sullenberger ("Sully") was an Air Force pilot before flying for decades as an airline pilot. He is part of a profession whose members are known for the ability to perform flawlessly, regardless of the degree of pressure they may experience. Sully and his first officer, Jeffrey Skiles, skillfully maneuvered a commercial airliner that had become a glider almost immediately after takeoff to a safe landing on the Hudson River. They did something that they had never done before and will never do again. And yet they were prepared—prepared to do the extraordinary.

You are now equipped with an array of tools that will allow you to reap maximum benefit from the concepts presented in this book. Remember that they are as applicable to your personal life as they are to your business life.

Congratulations. You have just earned your own wings of leadership!

Acknowledgments

We wish to extend our extreme gratitude to each of you who helped, encouraged, and otherwise inspired us to complete this heartfelt endeavor. The journey has been as enjoyable as the satisfaction of completing the project, in that it has allowed us to deepen our relationships with so many of you. Along the way, you patiently listened as we enthusiastically discussed the concepts as they evolved. You offered wise counsel and crucial input. From the CEOs, to our friends and family, and everyone in between, who were kind enough to offer feedback, we thank you for nudging us in one direction or another. We never could have done this without each and every one of you.

We would especially like to thank our editor, Daniel Seidel, for guiding us through the labyrinth of the countless rules of grammar in the English language.

Finally, we want to thank our dear parents for their selfless devotion to family, and the things that really count in life.

Glossary

GLOSSARY OF SELECTED TERMS

ACADEMICS
The non-flying part of Undergraduate Pilot Training (UPT) that consists of classroom instruction.

ACCIDENT INVESTIGATION BOARD
A board that is convened to investigate accidents. Its members have various areas of expertise including everything from engineering to psychology to aviation.

AEROBATICS
Maneuvers performed by aircraft that include loops, barrel rolls, aileron rolls, et cetera.

AEROBRAKE
After landing, raising the nose of an aircraft and using wind resistance against the fuselage (body) of the aircraft to assist in reducing its speed.

AFTERBURNERS
A section of a jet engine that provides for a tremendous increase in thrust. Found on high-performance trainer and fighter-type aircraft.

AIR FORCE ACADEMY
An institution of higher learning located in Colorado Springs, Colorado. Those who graduate earn a four-year bachelor's degree and become commissioned officers.

AIR TRAFFIC CONTROL

Generic term that may be applied to various agencies that monitor aircraft and give information and instructions via radio to pilots. Examples include Departure Control, Approach Control, Ground Control, and airport towers.

AIR TRAFFIC CONTROL TOWER

See Air Traffic Control.

AIRCRAFT LOGBOOK

A manual that contains information about a particular aircraft. Pilots also enter information in the logbook that requires the attention of maintenance personnel.

ALTITUDE

Aircraft height above the ground is called altitude, usually expressed in feet above Mean Sea Level, MSL, such as 10,000 feet MSL. Altitudes above 18,000 feet are often referred to as Flight Levels. For example, 24,000 feet could be expressed as Flight Level 240.

APPROACH

A way to align the aircraft with a runway. A visual approach is flown when a pilot uses ground references to proceed to an airport. An instrument approach is flown by reference to instruments and there is no requirement to be able to see the ground while en route to an airport.

APPROACH CONTROL

A part of the Air Traffic Control system that provides traffic separation and course guidance to pilots via radio transmissions.

BIRD STRIKE

A collision between a bird and an aircraft. Extreme cases can result in the loss of all engine power. Birds can also penetrate the windshield of an aircraft and cause severe injuries to a pilot.

BLUE ANGELS

The United States Navy Jet Demonstration Team.

BOLDFACE

Procedures that must be memorized and recited verbally or written with 100 percent accuracy.

BRAKE SYSTEM

An aircraft system that stops the wheels. Jet aircraft have antiskid systems that allow a pilot to apply full brake pressure, and computers control the brakes to prevent them from locking the wheels and causing a skid.

BREAKING OUT

In a traffic pattern, the term means a pilot is deviating from established procedures and leaving the pattern, usually because there is not adequate spacing from other aircraft. In formation flying, it means a pilot is taking his aircraft out of the formation. In the case of formation, pilots often do this if they lose sight of other aircraft in the formation.

BUFFETING

The shaking and vibrating of an aircraft that is associated with the disruption of airflow over the wing.

BUST

Slang term for failing an event, such as a checkride or test.

CANOPY

The clear windscreen on the top of an aircraft.

CHAIR FLYING

For pilots, a term used to describe simulating aircraft procedures while sitting in a chair.

CHECK PILOT

In Undergraduate Pilot Training (UPT), an Instructor Pilot (IP) assigned to Check Section, whose job it is to administer checkrides (see below) to UPT students.

CHECK SECTION

A small unit of pilots, usually seven to ten, charged with administering progress checkrides to UPT students.

CHECKLIST

A list of items to check or verify. Checklists are extremely important to pilots as they allow them to complete all required procedural steps, especially during emergency and stressful situations. Pilots also use checklists to accomplish normal procedures.

CHECKRIDE

A formal evaluation administered in an aircraft or simulator.

CHIEF OF CHECK SECTION

The commander of the small unit of checkpilots whose job it is to administer progress checkrides to UPT students.

CLEARED FOR APPROACH

The radio call a controller uses to authorize a pilot to fly an approach to an airport.

CLOSED APPROVED

The radio call that a controller uses when authorizing a pilot to fly a closed pattern.

CLOSED PATTERN

A small, tight pattern in the sky flown by high-performance aircraft when they are practicing takeoffs and landings.

CLOSURE RATE

The rate at which one aircraft is approaching another. This is a term commonly used in formation flying.

COMMISSIONED

A status in the military that refers to rank. Air Force officers receive a "commission" after they graduate from either the U.S. Air Force Academy, Officer Training School (OTS), or the Reserve Officer Training Corps (ROTC).

CONFIGURATION

The position of the gear and flaps on an aircraft. When both the gear and flaps are up, it is referred to as a "clean" configuration. When gear and flaps are down, it's called a "dirty" configuration.

CONTACT CHECKRIDE

A checkride that evaluates a pilot's ability to fly visually and perform aerobatics.

CONTACT FLYING

Flying by referring to outside references versus flying by reference to cockpit instruments.

CONTROL TOWER

A tower located on an airport from which Air Traffic Controllers issue instructions and clearances to pilots.

CONTROLLER

One who works at an Air Traffic Control facility such as a Control Tower, Approach Control or Departure Control.

CRABBING

When an aircraft turns to angle into the wind to maintain a desired ground track.

CROSSCHECK

Monitoring various instruments.

DC ELECTRICAL SYSTEM

A part of the electrical system of an aircraft that operates via Direct Current, versus Alternating Current (AC).

DEBRIEF

A discussion of what transpired on a flight. Also, end-of-chapter discussions in this book.

DEGREES OF BANK

The angle of the wings when an aircraft is in a turn. At 90 degrees one wing is pointing straight up, the other is pointing straight down.

DEPARTURE CONTROL

A part of the Air Traffic Control system that regulates aircraft as they depart an airport. Pilots talk to departure controllers via radios.

DEPARTURE COURSE

A course that a pilot flies after taking off from an airport. Pilots can define the course with their cockpit instruments or they can receive heading instructions from Air Traffic Control over the radio, which are called Radar Vectors.

EMERGENCY

A non-normal event or situation that could result in loss of life or aircraft damage.

FINAL APPROACH

The last segment of an approach that pilots fly when arriving at a runway.

FINGERTIP

In formation flying, this means flying extremely close to another aircraft and matching its every move.

FIRE LIGHT

A cockpit indication of an engine fire, usually a red light accompanied by an audible warning.

FIREWALL POWER

A term used to describe full engine power.

FLAP LEVER

A lever in the cockpit that sets the position of the wing flaps.

FLAPS

Located on the aft portion of a wing, they extend and thereby make the wing larger, provide increased lift, and allow an aircraft to fly at a slower speed. Flaps are typically lowered for takeoffs and landings.

FLIGHT COMMANDER

In pilot training, the commander of a particular group of pilot training students.

FLIGHT LINE

A term used to refer to where aircraft are parked and/or to squadrons that are located in the vicinity.

FLIGHT SUIT

Special overall-type suits made of fire-resistant material and worn by military pilots.

FLIGHT MATE

Student pilots within the same training unit, called a flight. Same as classmate.

FLYING PROFICIENCY

A pilot's ability to perform specific flight maneuvers.

FORMATION CHECKRIDE

A flight evaluation that tests a pilot's ability to fly formation.

FORMATION FLYING

Intentionally flying in close proximity to another aircraft. See "fingertip formation."

Gs

A term used to express the force of gravity exerted upon an aircraft and pilot during certain types of maneuvering.

G-SUIT

A bladder-filled specialized garment that a pilot wears to control blood flow throughout the body during high G-loads. A G-suit increases a pilot's tolerance of the force of gravity. The T-38 is rated to withstand approximately 7.33 Gs.

GLIDEPATH

A specified descent gradient on final approach, expressed in degrees. A three degree glide path equates to the requirement of an aircraft to descend 300 feet for every nautical mile flown.

GO-AROUND

To discontinue an approach.

GROUND EVALUATION

An oral examination in which an instructor or check pilot asks questions to determine the extent of a pilot's knowledge about certain aircraft systems and procedures.

GROUNDED

A term used by pilots to indicate a non-flying status.

GUSTY WINDS

Winds that change in intensity and direction very rapidly.

HAND SIGNALS

Pilots use hand signals to communicate with ground personnel, or other pilots during formation flying.

HEADING

The compass direction that an aircraft is flying or tracking toward.

HOLDING

A particular pattern that an aircraft flies in the event of a delay. The typical holding pattern flown looks like a racetrack, and has defined dimensions.

"I HAVE THE AIRCRAFT"

A phrase used when one person in a two-person aircraft takes or receives control of the aircraft. In pilot training, this is frequently done between student and instructor.

INITIAL

A position in the traffic pattern when a pilot flies directly overhead the runway prior to making a turn that will enable the aircraft to slow down and line up for a landing.

INSTRUMENT CHECKRIDE

An evaluation of instrument procedures administered in an aircraft or simulator.

INSTRUMENT FINAL

The final portion of an instrument approach.

INSTRUMENT FLYING
Flying by referring primarily to cockpit instruments instead of looking outside the aircraft and using visual references.

IP
Instructor Pilot.

KNOTS
Nautical miles per hour. A measurement of speed that is 1.15 times the miles-per-hour value.

LIMITATION
A procedural or system restriction.

LOGBOOK
A pilot's logbook is a book into which a pilot records details of a flight such as date, time, duration, et cetera. An aircraft logbook is a document that remains in the aircraft and in which pilots record details of a flight and maintenance issues that require attention.

LSU
Life Support Unit. The room in which pilots store their parachutes, helmets, et cetera.

MACH 1, Mach One
The speed of sound.

MISSING MAN FORMATION
A formation of aircraft flown usually as a tribute to a fallen aviator. Often the formation consists of four aircraft. When the formation flight arrives

directly overhead where the services are being held, a single aircraft pulls up and away from the rest, representing the departed aviator.

MORNING STAND-UPS
In UPT, verbal "what if" scenarios that are posed by an instructor pilot and must be answered and resolved by student pilots. If they fail to provide an acceptable solution to the presented situation, they can be removed from the flying schedule for a day.

NAVIGATION CHECKRIDE
An evaluation of a pilot's ability to fly, using instruments between two locations.

NOMEX
A type of fire-resistant material.

NOSE WHEEL STEERING
Turing an aircraft by manipulating the front, or nose wheel of an aircraft.

O' CLUB
Short for Officer's Club.

ON THE GO
A radio call made by a pilot who is visually discontinuing an approach.

OTS
Officer Training School. In the United States Air Force, a ninety-day school that leads to a commission as a second lieutenant.

OVERSPEED

Exceeding the maximum permissible speed for something. For example, the maximum speed to fly with full flaps extended might be 240 knots. Flying faster than 240 knots with full flaps extended would constitute an overspeed and the event would have to be written up in the aircraft logbook.

PATTERN ALTITUDE

A designated altitude that all aircraft must fly at a particular airport.

PERSONAL LOGBOOK

See Logbook.

PITCHOUT AND REJOIN

A maneuver practiced by aircraft flying formation. The purpose is to gain separation between two aircraft so they can practice getting back together, or "rejoining." Often the lead aircraft will initiate an aggressive turn, and his wingman will follow after a pre-determined delay, for example after waiting four seconds.

PRE-BRIEF

A discussion that takes place before a flight wherein pilots talk about what will take place during the flight.

PREPARTORY COMMAND

In formation flying, a visual command given that indicates a command of execution will follow. For example, the pilot in the lead aircraft of a formation will give a certain signal that he is about to lower his gear. His wingman will then pay close attention and will also lower his gear when the execution command is given.

RADAR VECTORS
When Air Traffic Control assigns the pilot of an aircraft a specific heading to fly.

RE-CHECK
A checkride that is given after a failed checkride.

ROTC
Reserve Officer Training Corps.

RSU
Runway Supervisory Unit. Similar to a mini control tower that is positioned next to a runway. An instructor pilot monitors and controls aircraft from the RSU via radio communications.

SA
Situational Awareness. Having an awareness of the "big picture."

SCENARIO
In pilot training, "what if" situations that are posed to students for which they have to determine a solution. See Morning Stand Ups.

SCHEDULER
The person who assigns instructors (IPs) and students to fly particular training missions.

SCHEDULING BOARD
The place where flying schedules are posted.

SHORT FINAL
The very end portion of an approach to a runway.

SIE
Self-Initiated Elimination. When a student pilot voluntarily quits pilot training.

SIMULATOR
A training device that is located on the ground. Sophisticated versions are extremely realistic and provide an environment in which pilots can practice virtually any procedure.

SINGLE-ENGINE GO-AROUND
Discontinuing an approach and flying on one engine (of a two engine aircraft) during the procedure. Also see Go-Around.

SINGLE-ENGINE LANDING
The T-38 has two engines. There are circumstances when it will perform a landing with only one engine, either due to the failure of an engine or the simulated failure of an engine for training purposes.

SOF (Supervisor of Flying)
A senior instructor who monitors the radios and is available to assist when there is a critical or emergency situation.

SOLO
A student flying without an instructor.

SORTIE
Commonly used as another term for mission or a single flight.

SPEED BRAKE

A device that extends from an aircraft that is designed to slow it down rapidly or increase its rate of descent.

SPEED OF SOUND

The speed that sound waves travel through the air.

SQUADRON

A group of pilots, with a common mission, who generally fly the same type of aircraft.

SQUADRON SAFETY OFFICER

Usually the additional duty of a pilot whose job it is to inform other pilots of current safety issues.

STALL SERIES

In UPT, practicing what to do in the event of a stall. A stall is the disruption of airflow over the wings. An additional type of stall is called a Compressor Stall. A Compressor Stall has to do with the disruption of airflow through a jet engine.

STAND-DOWN ORDER

Typically when a commander orders a halt in flying for a given period of time. Usually the result of an accident that has recently occurred.

STAND-UPS

See Morning Stand Ups.

STICK-AND-RUDDER

A pilot is considered a good stick-and-rudder pilot if he/she has good basic flying skills.

STRAIGHT-IN
Flying directly to a runway as opposed to flying a rectangular pattern to get aligned with the landing runway.

STRUCTURAL DAMAGE
Damage to an aircraft that may affect how it flies or handles.

SUBSONIC
Less than the speed of sound.

SUPERSONIC
At or beyond the speed of sound.

SYLLABUS
In UPT, a training schedule or plan.

T-37
Primary jet training aircraft. In UPT, it used to be the first aircraft student pilots flew. T-37s are being replaced by high-performance propeller aircraft.

T-38
Advanced, supersonic jet training aircraft. Also known as the White Rocket.

TAIL NUMBER
Individual aircraft identification number painted on the tail of an aircraft.

TASK SATURATION
The inability to process any new information.

THROTTLE
A lever, or similar, that controls fuel to the engine and thus engine output.

THUNDERBIRDS
The United States Air Force Aerial Jet Demonstration Team.

TIGER FLIGHT
In our story, the name of the training unit to which the student pilots belong.

TOP STICK
Best pilot.

TRAFFIC PATTERN
The organized pathway in the sky that aircraft fly around airports as they maneuver to land.

TRAINING AREA
In UPT, geographically defined areas in which pilots fly their aircraft for training purposes.

TWEET
Nickname for the primary basic jet trainer, the T-37.

UNDER THE BAG
Slang term for flying solely by instruments in the T-38. Students sit in the rear cockpit and pull a bag forward that completely obscures their outside visual references. It simulates flying in the clouds, or under instrument conditions.

UNEVENTFUL

A term used when an event is completed without consequence or difficulty. For example, a normal landing would be referred to as uneventful.

UPT

Undergraduate Pilot Training.

VECTORS

See Radar Vectors.

VISUAL STRAIGHT-IN

Flying an aircraft directly to a runway using visual references as opposed to using instruments for navigation to a runway.

WASHOUT

In UPT, failing to meet standards and being eliminated from the program.

WHITE ROCKET

Nickname for the T-38.

WINGS-LEVEL

Straight flight when the aircraft is not turning.

WRITE-UP

An entry in an aircraft logbook of a discrepancy or problem that a pilot requests a mechanic investigate.